THE SELF-EVALUATING INSTITUTION

Practice and Principles in the
Management of Educational Change

THE SELF-EVALUATING INSTITUTION

Practice and Principles in the Management of Educational Change

Clem Adelman and *Robin J. Alexander*

Methuen
LONDON and NEW YORK

First published in 1982 by
Methuen & Co. Ltd
11 New Fetter Lane, London EC4P 4EE

Published in the USA by
Methuen & Co.
in association with Methuen, Inc.
733 Third Avenue, New York, NY 10017

Printed in Great Britain at the
University Press, Cambridge

British Library Cataloguing in Publication Data
Adelman, Clem
   The self-evaluating institution.
   1. School management and organization
   I. Title   II. Alexander, Robin
   371.2'07   LB2901
ISBN 0–416–32740–0
ISBN 0–416–32750–8 Pbk

Library of Congress Cataloguing in Publication Data
Adelman, Clem.
   The self-evaluating institution.

   Includes bibliographical references and index.
   1. Educational accountability – Great Britain – Case studies.   2. Educa-
tion, Higher – Great Britain – Aims and objectives – Case studies.   I.
Alexander, Robin.   II. Title.
LB2901.A74 1982   379.1'54   82–8114
ISBN 0–416–32740–0   AACR2
ISBN 0–416–32750–8 (pbk.)

CONTENTS

ACKNOWLEDGEMENTS

My colleague, Ian Gibbs, was party to many of the experiences that are recounted in the 'Enlands' case section of this book. Without his genial company and greater faith in human kindness than mine, our tribulations would not have been turned until optimistic facets appeared.

John Barnett, Tom Eason, Colin Fox, Peter Hamilton and Lawrence Taylor were constant in their support of our attempts to foster institutional self-evaluation. I thank them and admire their efforts.

The research project, which was initiated by James Porter, was developed by Peter Seaborne, and funded by the Department of Education and Science. My thanks to the project steering committee for their judicious consideration of the project's products over the course of the two years. Pauline Perry took the tiller towards the end of the voyage and appreciated the project's attempts to address actual and potential issues of policy formation.

The emotional strength and lucid interpretations of my wife sustained the will to continue.

I want to thank Geoff Squire and his colleagues for permission to include an extract from the evaluation of their geography course.

CLEM ADELMAN

The 'Charlesford' evaluation was an integral part of college life during the period in question: thanks are therefore extended to the entire community of staff and students, all of whom were in some way involved in the programme.

Particular thanks must be recorded as follows. The Social Science Research Council funded part of the evaluation programme. Olive Coughlan was a tireless secretary. Len Wharfe provided necessary managerial support at critical stages. John Crick and Alan Young together undertook the 'portrayal' evaluation, one as evaluator, the other as willing subject.

Beyond Charlesford I gained much from discussions with Allan Rudd, from my *Evaluation Newsletter* colleagues Roland Hoste,

Judith Hargreaves and David McNamara, and, most recently, from exploring with David Billing and Brian Gent at the CNAA the evaluation issues generated by the CNAA's *Partnership in Validation* proposals.

Three people deserve special thanks. Pauline Harris, as the Charlesford evaluation programme's research assistant, did much of the hard work of instrument development, data analysis and report writing (some of which is exemplified in the chapter 3 case material). Aubrey Black, as chairman of the Charlesford evaluation committee, carried a major responsibility for the programme's operation but his consistent support and rare insight extended well beyond these particular circumstances. And my wife inevitably shared or endured much of the extended and difficult experience of first practising evaluation, then reconceptualizing and writing about it.

ROBIN ALEXANDER

INTRODUCTION

Origins and purposes

This book is the product of our endeavours to promote collective self-evaluation in two educational institutions and to understand, analyse and draw lessons from these experiences which might have general application. The projects which we draw upon for our examples and analysis were independently conceived and conducted, one ('Charlesford') starting in 1974 and the other ('Enlands') in 1975. Becoming acquainted during the course of this work, we found that despite the differences in approach and context there were notable problems and issues in common. Not the least of these was the novelty, for British educational institutions at least, of what we were undertaking. Each of us had searched the literature in the mid-1970s but had found very little to guide us. Each of us had written to and visited other institutions but had found that we were attempting something more ambitious than most had been prepared to try. At that stage institutional self-evaluation (or 'appraisal', or 'monitoring') seemed, if not unheard of, then more talked about or aspired to than actually practised.

We also found that while the literature on *evaluation* as such was by then quite extensive, it was almost exclusively contextualized in external consultancy evaluations, such as those conducted for Schools Council curriculum projects, where the problems were very different from those we faced, and where the bulk of the analysis not specific to those contexts, concerned questions of method and technique (Tawney, 1973; Eraut, 1976). By contrast our work showed each of us from a very early stage that the key challenges in institutional self-evaluation were interpersonal, political and organizational, rather than methodological, and that in any case evaluation methodology was itself institutionally constrained in all sorts of ways. This being so, we have chosen to concentrate on the contextual aspects of evaluation in this book, though we also include discussion of methods, and attempt to show (in chapters 5 and 6) how there is an underlying and shared epistemological dimension to both educational decision-making and educational evaluation.

We have found it necessary, in order to demonstrate the contextual embeddedness of institutional self-evaluation, to draw eclectically upon and juxtapose ideas from literature conventionally treated as distinct, even unrelated: notably, alongside evaluation, educational management, curriculum development and innovation, case study research and accountability. Sometimes we could apply this disparate material to our situations and problems, but often we found the lack of close attention to life within educational institutions a deficiency. For example, much material currently available on accountability, very much an 'issue' for the late 1970s and early 1980s, deals solely with the accountability of whole institutions to outside bodies — 'public accountability' — rather than with what to us is equally pressing, the accountability relations and obligations of groups and individuals *within* educational institutions to each other: pressing, especially, at a time when institutions are being forced to contract and this necessitates decisions by somebody, somewhere, about which staff or departments should stay, which should go, which should be merged.

In writing this book we draw not only on the Charlesford and Enlands evaluations and on the diverse literature indicated briefly above, but also on our combined yet very different careers and interests so far in education. Between us we have encompassed teaching, course planning, course administration and research in nearly every part of the education system: primary, secondary, further and higher, and the latter in its various institutional forms — college of education, college of higher education, polytechnic, university. We have separately researched the contingent higher education areas of evaluation, validation and institutional organization and decision-making. One of us has been since 1975 closely involved with the work of the country's major validating body, the Council for National Academic Awards (CNAA). We reckon this combined experience to be sufficiently comprehensive for us to argue with some conviction that although the actual cases cited in this book are from one part of the education system, our analysis and perspectives on institutional self-evaluation can provoke constructive discussion and be of practical use in a wide variety of institutional settings.

We recognize that we have theorized about the practice of evaluation in ways readers will want to question, and in particular the discussion in chapters 5, 6 and 7 may be disputed. It is our hope and intention that the book will provoke exactly this sort of reaction, for we share a view of educational issues as inherently open and debatable, and particularly so the issue, so often ignored or suppressed, of how an educational institution should itself go about the business of appraising, debating and improving its own practices. We would also hope that readers will feel inclined to bring to bear their own analyses, explanations and commentaries on the case material we provide, and to aid or provoke this we have included substantial detail and illustration in the two 'case study' chapters, 3 and 4.

Authorship

The book as a whole is a joint enterprise and certain sections have been jointly written. However, the distinctiveness and independence of the two projects which gave rise to our collaboration, and our separate publications in this and related fields, have necessitated elsewhere a clearer separation of author responsibility.

Chapter 1 is joint, though the distinction between different types of evaluation, the analysis of key decisions in the evaluation process and the models of accountability extend ideas from Alexander (1978a and 1980b) and Alexander, Billing and Gent (1980). An earlier discussion of some of the ideas dealt with here appears in Adelman and Alexander (1981).

Chapter 2 The 'Enlands' section is by Clem Adelman and the 'Charlesford' section by Robin Alexander. Some of the latter is expanded from parts of Alexander (1978b and c).

Chapter 3 is by Robin Alexander and uses material from his 'Charlesford' evaluation, some of which appears in that programme's SSRC research report (Alexander and Harris, 1977), some in unpublished 'Charlesford' documents.

Chapter 4 was written by Clem Adelman. It consists of unpublished material based partly on the experience of the evaluative research project at Enlands and partly on subsequent developments at the college.

Chapter 5 was written by Robin Alexander and draws on our joint analysis.

Chapter 6 brings together discussion of pluralism, evaluation methods and accountability (Robin Alexander), innovation strategies and the evaluator role (Clem Adelman).

Chapter 7 was written by Robin Alexander and draws on our joint analysis.

1 INSTITUTIONAL EVALUATION: DEFINITIONS, PRACTICES AND ISSUES

What is evaluation?

This book is about formal evaluation in and of educational institutions. By 'educational evaluation' we mean *the making of judgements about the worth and effectiveness of educational intentions, processes and outcomes; about the relationships between these; and about the resource, planning and implementation frameworks for such ventures.*

An educational institution's inhabitants are engaged in a more or less constant process of evaluation: every decision demands it, from matters of overall policy to a teacher's decisions about what to say or do at a particular point in time in the process of classroom events and relationships. Much of this evaluation is an extension into the everyday work of educators of those continuous appraisals of conditions and events on the basis of which humans act and interrelate. At this level, the evaluative process remains largely idiosyncratic and private, though none the less valid, and as far as the quality of educational experiences available to the student is concerned, this level of evaluation is probably the most potent. So one way of characterizing the range of evaluation processes is to place such appraisal at one end of a continuum ranging from 'informal' to 'formal', with evaluation programmes set up for specific purposes as a part of institutional policy at the other. However, informal evaluation contributes to formal evaluation in a variety of subtle and significant ways to the extent that whatever our professional determination to produce 'objective' judgements on students, courses or other educational or institutional phenomena, it is virtually impossible for such judgements to escape its influence. Informal evaluations may be the product of attributes, behaviours and values whioh are as much 'personal' as 'professional', and these influences can and do play a significant part at all levels of evaluation, regardless of the appearance of detachment and objectivity which many 'formal' evaluation procedures have or at least claim.

'Formal' evaluation, therefore, is distinct from 'informal' not so much in terms of judgemental process itself as by virtue of the *accessibility* of that process, the intentions which lie behind it and the uses to which it is put. By formal educational evaluation we mean the making of judgements of the worth and effectiveness of educational endeavours at a *public* level, sometimes as a matter of *deliberate institutional policy*. These judgements are ostensibly informed by criteria and methods which are to some degree open to scrutiny and appraisal in order that the judgements may reasonably claim to be valid and fair.

From practice to a theory for institutional evaluation

This book is grounded in our experiences as two agents of institutional evaluations. We describe and compare the evaluation programmes for which we were each responsible as a way of identifying the dilemmas involved for institutions engaging in evaluation, and in particular for those who occupy the critical roles in relation to such evaluation, whether these be evaluators, course managers, college administrators, teachers or students. From these accounts and discussions of particular events, we move towards a 'theory' for institutional evaluation which encompasses in a generalizable way what we take to be the key issues, problems, challenges and possibilities of evaluation in any sizeable educational institution. Thus, although some of this book deals with the particular problems of evaluators, much of what we say addresses the broader and far more important problem of how institutions might organize themselves for evaluation and self-evaluation, and suggests how they might acquire and make effective use of evaluative information to modify and improve institutional practices. As the reader will discover, we have views to offer about the sorts of institutional culture and organization which seem to be most conducive to adaptation and change. Above all, it is the very concepts of 'innovation', 'evaluation' and 'management' which underpin taken-for-granted everyday practices which most merit re-appraisal.

We hope that what we have to say will be of interest and use to staff in those institutions which more and more are being held accountable to outside bodies, but at the same time, regardless of external pressures, genuinely seek to evaluate and improve the quality of their educational and organizational practices as a contribution to institutional and professional growth and development. We believe that this book will be of interest to those professionally involved in curriculum and staff development and to students and practitioners of institutional evaluation and research.

Evaluation and institutional life

In theory *all* formal evaluations in an educational institution have in some way to do with furthering the stated educational purposes of the institution. However, for most staff certain evaluations are more obviously tied to these purposes than are others, and for this reason it is convenient to distinguish between evaluations made as a basis for *institutional* decision-making and policy formulation in general and those made as a basis for *educational* decision-making in particular. In the latter category we would distinguish three distinct sorts of formal evaluation common in educational institutions:

1 The appraisal of the quality and feasibility of course proposals or curriculum packages and the intentions and aspirations embodied within them. Where such appraisal leads to a decision about whether a proposal may be translated into action, we term it *validation*, and it can be undertaken by agents internal or external to the institution. (See Church, 1982.)

2 The appraisal of student performance on a course, especially, but not essentially, in relation to intended learning outcomes. This we term *assessment*. (See Heywood, 1977; Bloom *et al.*, 1971.)

3 The appraisal of a course's organization and teaching–learning processes in action, and its various outcomes (in addition to student learning). This is the usual sense in which *course* or *curriculum evaluation* is used. The most familiar form of course evaluation is the 'student feedback' approach, or survey of customer reaction (Dressell, 1976; Kemmis *et al.*, 1978; Flood-Page, 1977.)

Three points should be immediately apparent from this analysis. The first is that as formal processes *validation* and *assessment* are much more familiar forms of evaluation in institutions than is *course evaluation* (and in universities student assessment may be the *only* formal appraisal of a department's educational activities which takes place). The second is that the three are equally necessary and complementary elements in a comprehensive approach to institutional self-appraisal since one focusses mainly on intentions, another mainly on processes and another mainly on outcomes. Conceptually it would seem strange to try to make a case for only one or even two of these, rather than all three, to constitute an adequate basis for educational decision-making, yet in practice this is exactly what tends to happen: a college or polytechnic may be permitted under CNAA regulations to run a new course for five years purely on the basis of 'evaluations' of the adequacy of the claims made for it in advance; the same course may eventually be 'evaluated' on the basis of students' marks in examinations. In neither case is evidence sought about what *actually happens* on the course, about the interactions and processes central to learning.

The third point is that institutionally these three complementary parts of the evaluation process usually have separate and independent existences: this separation is both *organizational* in that there may be distinct bodies and procedures to deal with each (e.g. internal validation committees, course development groups, assessment/examination boards, evaluation units) and *temporal* in that they almost invariably follow a particular sequence — first plan, next validate, then teach, then assess, and finally evaluate. In the case of validation and assessment, the sequence is to some extent inevitable, but a justification for tacking course evaluation on at the end of the process of course development is hard to find. In practical terms it tends to ensure that data from one sort of evaluation is used only in relation to its immediate context (e.g. assessment data in relation to assessment procedures rather than, say, as commentary on teaching processes or course goals) and that the cross fertilization of judgements on proposals, student learning and courses in action can be very restricted. Decisions will then tend to be tied similarly to the immediate experiences of context, and the further separation of the elements as distinct and unrelated areas of institutional life will be exacerbated: decisions on planning, on assessment, on teaching methods etc. may be taken without significant reference to each other. Moreover, the extent to which these three facets of formal educational evaluation are institutionally and organizationally distinct may well reflect the demands for certain sorts of information, or for evidence that such information is being gathered, from external agencies to which an institution justifies its practices. In LEA sector higher education the character of internal institutional evaluation will reflect, in part at least, the requirements of validating bodies like the CNAA, and in this book we shall be concerned at certain points with what we see as a critical relationship between such external requirements and internal institutional responses in terms of policy and action.

Institutional self-evaluation is both *in* and *of* institutions. It is institutionally located and thus has a relationship to the complex network of norms, roles, values and relationships which make up the culture of an institution. And it is *of* institutions in that however particular the judgement — whether it is of a student, a course, a teacher or an educational proposal — it is in the end a judgement *of an institution's collective endeavour* to achieve the purposes for which it has been established. It is a conscious attempt to appraise this institutional endeavour and if it has any critical bite it will naturally produce reactions both positive and negative from individuals and groups involved or implicated.

Thus in the phrase 'institutional evaluation' the *institutional* dimension is as significant as the matter of *evaluation* techniques and criteria. In this book we shall reflect therefore not only on the latter but also on those key areas of institutional life to which they relate: curriculum innovation and institutional management. It is our assumption that improvements in these areas are unlikely without commitment to formal evaluation as a matter of policy. But we also believe, conversely, that the quality and usefulness of formal educational evaluations are very much dependent on the strategies and procedures for innovation and management. Consequently, it is necessary to explore the relationship between educational evaluation and other sorts of educational and institutional action in some detail.

Moreover, the ubiquitousness of public and private, formal and informal evaluations as elements in the life of educational institutions suggests strongly that the starting-point for the development of institutional evaluation policy must be *the explication and analysis of existing evaluation practices* rather than a grafting of new evaluation procedures onto an institutional culture whose existing evaluative processes remain unexplored and with which new policy and practice may prove incongruent. In certain instances it could well be that the most appropriate evaluation policy is an extension and integration of existing practices rather than additional arrangements.

Institutional self-evaluation in Britain

The practice of formal institutional evaluation of the sort that we discuss in this book has had limited development in Britain. In schools the practices may be private, unrecorded and unco-ordinated, reflecting the assumption that it is up to the individual teacher as professional to evaluate his own work; or they may entail collective school review through department, year or staff meetings. Sometimes the latter activity is supported (or started) by local education authorities, either through the initiatives of their advisers and inspectors, or through published school self-evaluation schedules of the sort used by Inner London (ILEA, 1977) or Salford (Salford Education Department, 1977). National bodies have also contributed to the development of school self-evaluation, either, in the case of the NFER, by producing highly formalized schemes for quantifying time-tabled curriculum events (Wilcox and Eustace, 1980) or by a looser and more comprehensive 'discussion document' approach, such as that offered by the Schools Council (1981) to counterbalance the increasing flow of bland and superficial pronouncements on the purposes and character of the school curriculum emanating from central government (e.g. DES, 1977, 1980 and 1981).

Generally, as we argue at various points in this book, evaluation processes reflect innovation strategies. In the 1960s and early 1970s the Schools Council fostered an approach to curriculum innovation dependent on a strategy of disseminating ideas and materials from centrally-based project teams to schools and teachers at the periphery. The relative lack of success of some of these projects prompted the Schools Council to change to a more localized strategy with support given for small-scale initiatives having a high degree of teacher involvement and school specificity. This shift is symptomatic of what is perhaps the most significant development for institutional self-evaluation at school level, the 'school-based'/'school-focused' movement, which is really a series of parallel but related movements, in professional consciousness, in curriculum development, evaluation, research and in-service education, all having in common a concern to enable the teacher to play a much greater part than hitherto in professional and curricular renewal. This movement manifests itself in action research by teachers (Nixon, 1981), owing much to the pioneering work of the Ford Teaching project (Elliott and Adelman, 1975, 1976; Adams, 1980), and in school-centred in-service education (Chambers, 1981; Alexander, 1980a), and the former in turn relates to the emergence of case study as a 'legitimate' mode of educational research (Simons, 1980) contrasting with the long-established experimental and survey traditions and reflecting a growing critique of strict positivism.

The richness and depth of these developments within and in relation to schools have no real parallel in higher education, where curriculum and pedagogy remain under-investigated, and institutionally-based educational evaluation tends to be restricted to the first two approaches we mentioned earlier: course proposal validation, and student performance assessment. There are of course exceptions, but they tend to be isolated and idiosyncratic rather than representative of discernible 'movements' of the sort which have emerged in connection with primary and secondary education. Moreover, such evaluations as have been reported tend to concern courses and teaching in vocational and scientific/technical subjects; if published evaluation studies are an accurate guide, arts and non-vocational courses receive little evaluation of the formal variety. There are, however, a number of research studies of higher education, which, while they do not qualify as 'institutional self-evaluations', throw some light on the chances of success of such activities.

One of the most extensive studies was that of the Nuffield Higher Education group, directed by Becher. This group looked into attempts at curriculum innovation and its consequences within universities and polytechnics, but despite the incisiveness of several of the interim reports the final report (Becher *et al.*, 1976) was, in our view, disappointing. It suggested that although the institutions of higher education that were studied were slow to take up and respond to innovation and generally ignored negative evaluation, they should be left to carry on in their own inimitable ways. Perhaps the authors of the final report were concerned about the pressures from government to make higher education institutions more accountable to a central authority, maybe the DES or through the UGC, with the implication of greater central definition in the distribution and differentiation of courses across higher education institutions.

ANABAS, a sub-project of the Nuffield Higher Education group, involved five universities which had agreed to some of their degree programmes being evaluated. The fieldworking evaluators came up against the problem that although the university administration had given general agreement for the work of the project, individual staff resisted the process of collection of data and there was sometimes considerable antagonism towards the project's reports.

The Sussex project described by Eraut, Connors and Hewton (1981) was more specifically concerned with how individuals might be trained to promote innovation in higher education institutions. Unlike the Nuffield group this project team studied teacher education institutions as well as polytechnics and universities. They found innovation in universities to be underdeveloped, or at the most privatized, and though there was a greater commitment to collective course improvement in the LEA-maintained institutions, systematic evaluation tended not to form a part of such activity.

One section of higher education — teacher education — has perhaps a stronger tradition of self-investigation, possibly because it straddles the very different worlds of schools and higher education and is in a state of more or less continuous identity crisis, or because many key figures in educational research are based in colleges/departments of education. The two projects on which this book draws (reported in Alexander and Harris, 1977; Adelman and Gibbs, 1979) stem from this tradition, as does the work of Hoste (1981, 1982) on course evaluation methodology. From the teacher-education base too has emerged the network of evaluation practitioners whose efforts have been reported in *Evaluation Newsletter* (CRITE 1976–9, CRITE/SRHE 1979–   ).

Evaluation and validation: the significance of the CNAA

However, what to us seems particularly significant for the development of coherent approaches to evaluation in higher education institutions is the influence on ideas and practices of the Council for National Academic Awards as the main validating body. Until recently, for institutions running CNAA-validated courses, there has been a clear distinction between 'internal' and 'external' validation. The latter is the activity undertaken by the CNAA whereby a course proposal and its staffing, resource and management contexts are assessed and, if found to meet certain criteria, are deemed 'validated' for a given period of time, thus enabling the course proposal to be translated into living educational events and relationships. (See Alexander and Wormald (1982) for a comparison of CNAA and university validation styles and criteria). Internal validation is a process, controlled and conducted by and within the institution, of 'vetting' a proposal before forwarding it in its polished form to an external validating agency (in the case of LEA maintained sector institutions) or to enable it to be put into operation (e.g. in a university, where, of course, all validation is 'internal'). In the latter case validation may be no more than a rubber-stamping formality at faculty or senate level which ensures that the outward forms of a proposal — title, syllabus and examination arrangements — are consistent with prevailing practice. In the former case something considerably more extensive is involved, and colleges may have systems for internally appraising proposals which are as rigorous as anything offered by an external body (Alexander and Gent, 1982). However, internal validation procedures may tend to exist not so much because they are seen as educationally desirable but because they are a proven device for maximizing the chances of successful *external* validation. This may distort the judgemental criteria so that they are less about the educational quality of the proposal than about its chances of being externally validated. Internal validation becomes a dummy-run for the 'real' validation rather than a process of appraisal deemed valuable in its own right. Moreover, the style of internal validations, being modelled on the real thing, tends to repeat the inadequacies of external validation. Thus they may display disproportionate concern with documents and claims (rather than actions), and the ability to present a convincing case: performance and pre-packaging skills (Alexander, 1979) may count for more than the case itself. What we have yet to see in higher education is a genuinely comprehensive procedure for appraising course documents and statements of intent comparable to those developed in connection with school curriculum materials (e.g. Eraut *et al.*, 1975).

For maintained-sector institutions of higher education this model of validation is now in the process of modification, following the publication of the CNAA's most recent *Partnership in Validation* proposals which introduce a greater measure of flexibility into the validation process and place greater reliance on institutions' internal procedures, both for the initial validation of courses and for their subsequent monitoring and evaluation (CNAA, 1975 and 1979a). Course approval will now be for indefinite periods, subject to regular reviews at five-yearly intervals, and reviews will consider not merely course proposals but also internal procedures for validating and evaluating such proposals (Kerr *et al.*, 1980). It is not yet clear what criteria or methods the CNAA will use for appraising the adequacy of these internal validation/evaluation procedures: at the time of writing colleges are being encouraged to bring forward their own suggestions for implementing the idea of 'partnership' to contribute to discussion within the CNAA. Since the publication of *Partnership in Validation* and *Developments in Partnership in Validation*, the CNAA has become closely concerned with the conduct and problems of 'institutional review', presumably as a consequence of its experience of visits to institutions and the responses that institutions have made to CNAA reports about their organization, staffing and curriculum. The CNAA's influence is substantial: it has power to withdraw validation of courses; its recommendations on how programmes might be administered and on appropriate organization and staffing are usually heeded by institutions. However, although the CNAA — like the DES — may issue recommendations for practice, both acknowledge that the institution knows more about itself than any outside body. Some go rather further and argue that it is 'impractical, unreal, impertinent and unprofessional' for the CNAA to expect to be able to make a valid judgement about the quality of an institution on the basis of its current procedures (Ball, 1981); it is partly in response to such criticisms that the CNAA has placed greater emphasis on institutional *self*-evaluation.

However, how much more 'valid' can be the institution's appraisal of itself? Requests for information about registry statistics, budgeting, formal organization and aspirations are familiar foci for external appraisal, but most institutions have limited knowledge, and this usually of an unsystematic kind, about the qualities of their programmes and courses as experienced by their students, and the problems and successes of teaching these courses as experienced by their staff. Although a considerable volume of opinion may be voiced in committees, senior common rooms and staff rooms, there are few occasions when systematic attempts are made to collect information which would allow the institution to debate the worth of particular pedagogic practices, courses and programmes.

The CNAA has now begun to work towards specifying the *criteria* that it will use to judge whether its validated institutions are able to make an appropriate 'self-analysis' (CNAA usage) of their practices, and this development seems highly significant not merely for the institutions directly affected, but — given the paucity of alternative models — for the theory and practice of institutional evaluation generally. Rather than concentrating on content and teaching the focus appears to be on management and resources (CNAA, 1980 and 1981). This is significant, as in our view the way in which management is conducted determines the 'health' (CNAA usage) of the institution as much as do the quality and adventurousness of the teaching. The crucial question is whether the way in which management is conducted is appropriate and/or effective in fostering the educational practices of the institutions. (This presupposes that management and teaching are manifest and acceptable as a division of labour). Here the CNAA might concede that industrial management by objectives and the bureaucratization of small institutions with a diversity of programmes have not necessarily been conducive to the fostering of educational qualities. In the criteria under the 'Objectives' section of *Notes for the Guidance of Institutions* (CNAA, 1980) the Committee for Institutions refers only to resources and management.

Given these requirements, what criteria will heads of departments, deans or directors of courses use to justify their endeavours? Those appropriate to profit-making organizations, or to the consumer base of education institutions? If the CNAA wishes to assure itself that the institution is 'healthy', what set of managerial phenomena will be taken as symptomatic of any disease? But, more significantly for self-accounting, does the institution have any ideas about the aetiology? The 'healthy' institution, on CNAA management criteria, will presumably be one that is capable of mounting courses of consistent quality.

It is not difficult to envisage the managers in many institutions trying to justify their endeavours by criteria such as efficiency of resource distribution and staff allocation. But that would not be sufficient for the CNAA as the managers would also need to demonstrate evidence. Yet the request that managers give accounts of their practices places them in positions of vulnerability in their own institutions if their accounts go beyond CNAA readership.

What can be evaluated, what is accessible and releasable, may be subject to the control of 'gatekeepers' (Barnes, 1979; Adelman, 1980; Alexander and Wormald, 1982), usually managers and committees. There are few institutions that allow the process of evaluation to open all the 'books' and release all reports (though see the Charlesford evaluation in the present book for an example of one such 'open' reporting policy in action), and it would be naïve for an institution not to be wary of the consequences of such release of information (Mac-

Donald, 1976b). There are no institutions without some conflict, usually factional, and the report that pleases one will not please another (Becker, 1970), even if the evaluation encompasses multiple realities and attempts to be just and fair. Differentials in power over other peoples' lives in institutions will continue to make institutional evaluation difficult to conduct.

An institution that conducted self-appraisal as an ordinary rather than a quinquennial activity would be pioneering in British higher education; though several higher education institutions in Sweden are currently exploring the possibilities of 'activity evaluation' (Furumark, 1979), while Braskamp (1980), Rippey (1975) and Dressel (1976) chart the sometimes substantial developments in faculty evaluation in the USA, using self-evaluation, peer evaluation and student ratings; we report some of the Swedish and American experiences in the next section. However, as Becher and Kogan (1980) state, 'formal evaluation is only a marginal aspect not an inherent feature of British higher education . . . higher education is as poor in impersonal evaluation as it is rich in personal judgement'. We consider that Becher and Kogan's statement 'institutions are not as knowledgeable about the specialisms which they collectively provide . . . academic judgement which an institition has to make in its basic units is made in a position of comparative ignorance' is both accurate as a commentary on current practice and disturbing when set in the context of the contraction of higher education now under way. On what evidence about the educational activities of departments are judgements and decisions about selective cuts to be based, given the paucity and superficiality of current knowledge?

The above discussion of the CNAA may seem somewhat parochial in a book aimed at a wider audience. However, the CNAA's significance in evaluation matters is not restricted to CNAA-validated institutions. Rather it is because in the absence of any significant tradition in higher education of explicit 'formal' course evaluation, the styles of evaluation engendered as a result of 'partnership' could provide the only available operational model for all manner of institutions at a time when internal evaluation seems the appropriate response to accountability pressures and budget cuts. It has frequently been suggested, for instance, that the quality of some university courses would be greatly improved if they were subject to CNAA-style validation (a suggestion emanating from within the universities — see Ball (1981) and Alexander (1979) — not merely from disgruntled victims of university members of CNAA validation panels). There are also suggestions that the CNAA's 'model' of validation could be translated into schools as a form of institutional self-evaluation to offset pressures for public accountability. One such case (Becher and Maclure, 1978, pp. 233–8) seems to us to rest on a serious failure to take account of the considerable limitations of the CNAA validation model (Alexander, 1979; Ball, 1981) and erroneously characterizes CNAA validation as being a device for appraising both educational processes and products, whereas it is pre-eminently a means for appraising *intentions*, only marginally (through external examiners' reports) a means of appraising products, and hardly at all a means of appraising processes. The 'CNAA model' would offer, as it stands, an extremely restricted basis for institutional self-evaluation.

Thus we would see the contribution of the CNAA's proposals as one to be welcomed in that they may encourage debate about institutional self-evaluation, but also as needing to be treated with caution because they may limit the extent of such debate. There is always the danger that the unique initiative may become a conceptual straitjacket; that the one available model may gain a monopoly. This has happened in the evaluation field before, most notably in the way the conceptual framework for evaluation has been dominated by the experiences of external consultancy project evaluations along Schools Council lines. Similarly, it is easy to assume only one available operationalization for 'validation'. Elsewhere it can mean something rather more extensive than intention appraisal: in British Forces establishments, for example, it connotes the approval of courses *which have demonstrated their success in action* over a trial period and have had the 'wrinkles' ironed out: something more akin, in fact, to what is termed in mainstream curriculum parlance 'summative evaluation'.

Comparisons: institutional evaluation in the USA and Sweden

It is instructive to compare the above account with practices and views of institutional evaluation as these have emerged in relation to higher education in the United States and Sweden.

Readers will probably be aware of the extent to which the curriculum and evaluation fields in Britain have derived considerable impetus — at least in terms of theory and methods — from the very substantial American literature, most obviously, perhaps, in relation to the debate about means–ends models of curriculum planning, the use of behavioural objectives and the polarizing of quantitative and qualitative evaluation and assessment methods. Such moves to make the planning and evaluation of educational activities more systematic and 'scientific' have been linked by writers like Kliebard (1974) and Eisner (1967, 1969, 1979) with utilitarian/cost-benefit views of education, and with consequent pressures for schools and colleges to demonstrate their accountability in terms of readily-measurable 'results' to external bodies. Inglis (1975) has offered comparable analyses of the British curriculum movement, locating the managerial/assembly-line concept of educational processes in the nineteenth-century utilitarian industrial and political context. The relationship between approach and broader context is important, not only because it is essential to retain a sense in general of how educational ideas are culturally embedded, but because, while the assembly-line model of curriculum and evaluation imported from the USA was viewed by many as strongly inconsistent with British educational ideology and practice in the affluent and liberal 1960s, the severe financial recession of the early 1980s has been associated with a strong swing back to a neo-Victorian utilitarianism which may give the earlier industrial models renewed currency and attractiveness to keepers of educational policy and finance at national and local levels.

In this context the more recent approaches to evaluation for institutional and faculty development in the United States reviewed by Braskamp (1980) offer important lessons. He suggests that in the USA evaluation has served three primary purposes: to help the individual instructor to improve as a teacher, to provide information for decisions about tenure, annual salary increases and responsibilities, and to provide information to students to enable them to select their courses. The second of these has been the area of greatest growth as a result of increased demand for certain sorts of information by administrators who have to make personnel decisions. However, evaluation to assist teacher improvement is the purpose most widely advocated by the educational community. The rhetoric has been that there should be a strong connection between faculty evaluation and development but unfortunately, in practice, the integration of evaluation and development is not always that strong. From his experience in the University of Illinois, Braskamp suggests that evaluative information must be fair, must be useful to intended audiences and the evaluation achieved should foster the initiatives by faculty members to become better self-evaluators. Braskamp advocates the 'multiple-source' approach to evaluation to meet the complexity of the teaching process and the different perceptions of it held by different people both inside and outside higher education, and to be consistent with the pluralism and diversity in American higher education. He advocates individual self-evaluation but particularly peer evaluations as means towards fair and valid evaluation information and argues that the key to peer evaluation is the development of a trusting relationship between colleagues. Colleague evaluation of actual classroom teaching seems most appropriate for the purpose of instructor development. Student ratings of teachers are suggested as of worth, particularly as these often reflect the unique features of the course. However, regardless of the means by which student feedback is gained, Braskamp observes that the staff have difficulty in handling negative comments.

Rippey (1975) reviews a range of student evaluation of teachers in higher education and suggests that student ratings can be meaningful and useful only in particularly limited contexts but that students can provide important information from the point of view of their lengthy experience with their teachers. Rippey argues that beginning or uninformed students are not in a position to judge the accuracy of course conditions and that student rejection of content as irrelevant or useless may have limited validity.

Braskamp (1980) and Dressel (1976) emphasize the crucial requirement that evaluations should be agreed to by staff and be seen as having potentially useful outcomes for improving courses, programmes and institutional practices. However, as Braskamp observes, since evaluation in higher education in the USA has tended in practice to be associated with the means by which administrators make decisions about tenure, promotion and other aspects of academics' careers, this makes it difficult for those who believe that evaluation can help to improve academic practices and management to offer a convincing case.

Such developments as those discussed by Braskamp have tended to be local. In view of the greatly increased exercise of direct central government intervention in schools and higher education which has occurred in Britain since 1979, it is useful to consider how another national system has attempted to reconcile central interest with grassroots needs and anxieties.

Since 1975, the National Swedish Board of Universities and Colleges has been conducting studies of innovation in higher education. In July 1977, after an Act passed by the Swedish Parliament, NSBUC was commissioned to monitor the consequences of de-centralized academic decision-making and the way budgets were spent within individual institutions. The Act also broadened access to higher education and gave the opportunity for institutions to participate in national development of higher education. NSBUC began five-year programmes of activity concerned with key aspects of innovation and its consequences, employing consultants, fieldworkers and administrators to engage in the research. The funds for this work have come from central government.

The reports (Berg and Oestergren, 1977; Furumark, 1980) which have emerged have concentrated mainly on case studies in smaller institutions away from the central focus of Stockholm. Several of the case studies that have been reported and referred to are based on work in the northernmost university in Sweden, others on smaller professional colleges, in areas of study other than natural science and technology.

The fieldworkers have aimed to foster institutional self-evaluation initially through what they term 'activity evaluation'. Activity evaluation is looked upon strictly as an 'internal affair' meant to provide a better basis for decisions that are taken by and within the institutions themselves:

> Activity evaluation should not be ordered to prescribe from above. It should be an enterprise initated and shaped by the institution's officers in order to serve their own internal needs for knowledge, insight and awareness concerning what they are doing, how well they do it and what it costs so they may raise their capacity for re-appraisal of priorities and re-direction of resources for renewal. (Furumark, 1980)

The reports make it explicit that NSBUC is aware of the tensions between being commissioned by government to look into the capacity of institutions to develop and the fostering of means for institutions to regulate their own activities. The smaller institutions, and particularly those away from the power base of Stockholm are, according to NSBUC, not only most vulnerable to shifts in the allocation of resources but are also more concerned about evaluating the consequences of their own academic policies, curriculum and teaching. The project is convinced that no one model can be developed to suit all the varying needs within the unified but still highly diversified system of higher education. In this connection, special attention is given to the smaller, newly-established colleges on the assumption that these institutions' activity evaluation has a particular role to play in their struggle for consolidation and development.

The reports of the project up to 1980 do not indicate the use that central decision makers have made of the case and other studies conducted through activity evaluation. Results of these have been published as they emerged so they may be used also as a basis for local decisions on desirable changes. Although the aspiration of the project is towards fostering institutional self-evaluation through activity evaluation with the information assisting the institution in its own appraisals, the need to report back to government on how the 1977 legislation is working requires considerable negotiation with individual institutions to release evaluation reports. These reports are required both in the interest of information sharing and in order, presumably, for the NSBUC researchers to demonstrate the quality of their work to the project commissioners.

□ *The process of activity evaluation*

The process of activity evaluation should be well planned and carefully structured so as to defend its place in a rationally functioning organization. When planning an activity evaluation project one should define the activity to be studied, decide on the purpose of the project, calculate costs and the time needed, distribute tasks and responsibilities and, above all, make absolutely clear how results will be reported and used.

We think it very important that as many as possible of those concerned — staff, students, administrators — should be involved in the process at an early stage. One should try to anticipate what problems are likely to arise and think of ways to handle them. Care should be taken to secure support for the project from those in power — rectors, governors and top administrators.

The process itself must begin by a description of all current activities in objective and quantitative terms. These will include not only student and staff numbers, courses, examination, budget etc. but also other frame factors that make up the conditions and constraints for the activities of the self-studying unit.

The next step would be to assess the 'quality' of what one is doing. That is, of course, the most crucial and conflict-laden part of

the process. Goals must be discussed, studied, derived, interpreted, accepted, discarded and reset. Value judgements will clash.
Criteria, indicators and measures must be developed and agreed
on.

This part of the activity evaluation is the very heart of the matter,
and too big and complicated to be dealt with here (even if we had
the expertise, which is not the case). We think that institutions and
departments will have to formulate their own goals, develop their
own criteria and their own methods to judge their activities. That
does not exclude that they may choose to invite outside expertise to
scrutinize and assess their performance. Peer review is an interesting method that is hardly ever used in Sweden. It deserves being
tried, e.g. in the form of two institutions agreeing to exchange
examination teams.

The final step of the evaluation process would be to indicate how
things should be, what changes should be made, what development
work undertaken, what programmes terminated, what ambitions
raised or lowered, etc. (Furumark, 1980)   □

The case studies reported in Berg and Oestergren (1977) illustrate the
complexities of activity evaluation but also how innovation leading to
subsequent changes in professions studied has been developed within institutions. The studies refer particularly to resistance to innovation and draw on the research and theorizing of writers like Lewin
(1948), Havelock (1977), and Schon (1971).

The Swedish project has adopted a pluralistic, non-interventionist,
multi-disciplinary approach. The rhetoric of the 1977 Act, of de-
centralization, broader student participation and democratic decision-making, has been monitored by the activity evaluations. From
the cases that are so far reported this activity evaluation (which has
many aspects in common with what we call 'institutional evaluation')
has been moderately successful within institutions but we have little
knowledge of its applicability and use nationally.

Accountability and the control of institutional evaluation

We argue in this book that those devising programmes and procedures
for institutional evaluation need to devote at least as much attention to
the character of their institution as to the methods by which its work
might be evaluated. The extent to which one sees the institutional

context as problematic for evaluation depends on one's analysis of institutional reality. We tend to conceive of educational institutions as places characterized by conflict and plurality, whatever impressions of order and consensus they might manage to give to outsiders or even to some of their own members. Rarely, we suggest, can one find a higher education institution having the unity of purpose and commitment implied by the encapsulating term 'institution', and in any case the strongly hierarchical structures of such institutions guarantee the existence of competing interests. This being so, 'institutional evaluation', cannot in any practical, comprehensive sense mean 'evaluation by an institution of itself and its activities' but rather it is generally a matter of *one part* of an institution evaluating *a limited range* of these activities.

Exactly what the activities are, and how they are evaluated, depends on who controls the evaluation. And since it is another basic premise of this book that, given the choice, most people would prefer not to have their professional work subjected to the public scrutiny implied by 'institutional evaluation', we infer further that control of the evaluation process is something to be prized, not least as a means of deflecting attention away from one's own activities.

What, more specifically, do we mean by control of evaluation? We see evaluation as encompassing a number of related decisions, as follows:

1 Decisions about *goals*. What is an evaluation for? What purpose is it to serve?
2 Decisions about *focus*. What aspects of institutional life, of courses, teaching, learning, administration etc. are to be evaluated?
3 Decisions about *methods*. By what means is information to be gathered on the basis of which evaluative judgements and possibly subsequent policy decisions are to be made?
4 Decisions about *criteria*. What will be the nature and source of the criteria to be used for judging the worth and/or effectiveness of the aspects of institutional life studied?
5 Decisions about *organization*. Who will undertake the evaluation? What resources will be available? How will the programme be organized?
6 Decisions about *dissemination*. To whom will the findings of evaluation studies be made available? What will be the extent of openness or confidentiality?

7 Decisions about *application*. To what use will evaluation studies be put? By what process will they feed into institutional decision-making?

Control of evaluation, then, is multi-faceted. However, our experience showed that not all these decisions and questions are perceived as being equally significant to all parties. To the Charlesford evaluation committee and the Enlands evaluators attention to *methods* and *criteria* was essential to preserve the integrity and the credibility of the process. To course managers what mattered more than these was control of *focus, dissemination* and *application*, of what to evaluate (and, especially, what to avoid evaluating), whom to make findings available to and what action to take in the light of such findings. In the Charlesford evaluation, control of all the decisions was invested by the constitution in the college academic board which, having agreed on *focus* and a standard *dissemination* policy left the details of *methods, criteria* and *organization* to the evaluation committee. But the final decision, about *application*, was delegated to the course management committees and they thereby retained a substantial measure of control of the entire process since without tangible applications to policy an evaluation programme soon loses its credibility.

Individual self-evaluation is a process of finding out about and judging one's own activities for one's own purposes. *Institutional* self-evaluation is the means by which individuals and groups find out about and judge their own and each other's activities as these contribute to the institution's *collective* endeavours. It is the tool of *accountability*. Now, conventionally, discussion of accountability tends to focus on extra-institutional relationships, on the 'public' accountability of whole institutions to outside bodies who have a claim to know how well they are performing.[1] Indeed, much institutional evaluation is devised to meet demands for such public accountability. But the process of institutional evaluation throws into sharp relief the issue of *internal* accountability, of who should be answerable to whom for what actions. We would suggest that control of the central evaluation decisions listed above is a vital means of determining the direction of the accountability relationship. Whoever controls the evaluation can control *de facto* this relationship regardless of the formalized *de jure* accounting relationships worked out for the institution — faculty boards, academic boards and the like. Thus, to take just one evaluation decision, a policy of confidentiality on the *dissemination* decision effectively ensures that those who are the subjects of an evaluation report become accountable to the limited few who are permitted to read that report rather than vice versa, and a policy of open dissemination to some extent ensures that there is greater likelihood of individuals and groups demonstrating accountability to each other. However, this in turn depends on control of the *focus* decision, for an open dissemination policy is effectively neutralized if only certain aspects of institutional life are studied and the work of some groups and individuals escapes scrutiny. Thus the *focus* decision in its way becomes as crucial as the *application* decision and the (wholly natural) tendency of bodies controlling evaluation is to avoid at all costs having their own work appraised.

So there need to be consistent procedures on control for all seven evaluation decisions, to ensure that none is invalidated by others, and that the accountability relationship is in reality what it is claimed to be: the Charlesford evaluation committee idea was an attempt to provide such procedures (though with what success we shall discuss later) as were the later evaluation policies at Enlands which grew out of the experiences described in chapter 4.

Models of accountability

The following 'ideal types' of accountability (adapted from Alexander, 1980b) reflect assumptions and practices currently obtaining in educational institutions and show how the accountability relationship is related to the location of control of the central evaluation decisions listed above.

1 *Professional autonomy* This model reflects the assumption that what goes on in a particular educational institution, course or classroom is the responsibility of each of the professionals concerned. It rests on a view of the individual — whether teacher, manager or administrator — as professionally competent over the full range of activities he undertakes, and this competence includes the necessary knowledge and skills to make or seek insightful and valid appraisals of his work and to act on those appraisals. His status as 'professional' is a guarantee of the integrity of such evaluation. The professional retains control over the key evaluation decisions of what to evaluate, how, to whom to disseminate findings and what

action to take in the light of them. We see this view as particularly pervasive at the departmental level of British universities, as ideology, if not always as practice, and to some extent as an assumption underpinning teaching at all points in our educational system. However, despite its pervasiveness, it is not properly a model for *institutional* self-evaluation since it is essentially the antithesis of that collective sense on which the latter depends.

2 *Managerial*   This model reflects the assumption that the individual is formally accountable to those who administer and control the course or institution to which he contributes and who allocate human and other resources to his work. What goes on in his classroom or office, therefore, is of legitimate concern to such 'managers' and control of the key evaluation decisions is vested in them as a function of their designated responsibility. This view, or its modified version which follows, appears particularly dominant in the further education /technical strand of non-university higher education (especially in the polytechnics).

3 *Consultative*   This model reflects the view that, as professionals, individuals in an institutional hierarchy have a right to be involved in discussions about their work but that the form of such involvement and the control of evaluation decisions still rests with 'managers'. It is the version of 'democratic' decision-making operated in many educational institutions and is a familiar response at local and national government levels to pressure for public 'participation' in decision-making.

4 *Mutual culpability*   This model reflects the view that all who participate directly in a particular educational activity have a legitimate interest in its quality and progress, that such quality and progress are the result of the particular contribution which each participating group or individual makes, and that, therefore, participants should account to each other for their various contributions. Being the most public and open form it is some distance from 'professional autonomy' at the individual teacher level, though in fact it is essentially a model for professional autonomy at the whole institution level. It does not necessarily incorporate any particular structural view of institutional decision-making (e.g. 'open' or 'participatory' in the sense of non-hierarchical); it allows for continued role and status-differentiation, such as is probably inevitable in both schools and higher education institutions. It is egalitarian only in the sense that it requires that all participants, regardless of

role or status, see themselves as equally accountable to each other for their particular contributions to the educational process. Control of the evaluation decisions rests with the participants, and in organizational terms steps have to be taken to prevent the domination of one group's definition of what is problematic, what is evaluation-worthy, or what are the 'facts' about the activities being evaluated. We see this model as likely to be reflected not so much in practices as in *aspirations* or *climate* in educational institutions.

5 *Proletarian*   This is the exact reverse of managerial accountability in that the accounting relationship is downwards from those given managerial responsibility to the 'workers'. At the same time it is neither a 'professional autonomy' model (since it is collectivist rather than individualist) nor 'mutual culpability' (since the accountability is one-way only). This, since it implies student and/or grass-roots staff control, is the least likely in the British educational context, but it is a theoretical possibility, and of course, like all the other models it has its counterpart, as a working out of the relationship of the individual to the state, in national political systems.

Note that no accountability model implies a particular organizational form for evaluation, except — probably — 'professional autonomy' which implies private self-evaluation and is therefore not a model for *institutional* self-study as such, however important it is to professional development at the deeper level. But even 'professional autonomy' could involve others: an individual could invite a colleague to observe and comment on his teaching, or could distribute a feedback questionnaire to students. What matters is that *he controls the key evaluation decisions* and so if his colleague or the questionnaire come up with unpalatable conclusions about his teaching he is not obliged to act on them or to divulge them to anyone else.

In this book we examine the control of evaluation, and the accountability relationships thereby implied in respect of the activities being evaluated; we also consider the matter of congruence between the control/accountability dimension of each of the main evaluation decisions and between these and related areas of academic decision-making, especially those concerned with course planning and management. For evaluation is but one sort of academic decision-making, and its quality and effect are critically dependent on the quality of decision-making in general in an institution.

In its turn an institution's overall decision-making tends to be explained or justified in terms of notions of 'efficiency' and 'democracy' (the latter being an ideal which most institutions of higher education feel obliged to endorse). There are many criteria of 'efficient' educational or managerial activity, and many versions of institutional democracy; our experience suggests that the process and products of evaluation make demands of an institution's members such that they need to develop an acute self-awareness about the claims and practices put forward in pursuit of each of these.

What is 'successful' evaluation?

In the next three chapters we describe the evaluation processes at 'Charlesford' and 'Enlands' colleges and juxtapose sample evaluation studies from the two programmes. These convey something of the diversity of the evaluation process — of foci, or issues which can be studied, of methods and criteria which can be used, of ways of reporting outcomes, of dissemination policies and of uses to which studies can be put: of ways, in other words, of taking the various evaluation decisions listed earlier, even within the limits of only two institutional programmes. The examples also provide case material which we hope readers will feel inclined to subject to their own analyses.

Some of the studies we report were clearly complex and for various reasons difficult. Some of them produced adverse or at least mixed reactions.

We see it as important to be honest about the difficulties in order that our experiences can be helpful to others. At the same time we should emphasize that 'success', 'failure', 'ease' and 'difficulty' are relative concepts and that in our view evaluation is not only inherently problematic but also necessarily so: if it is bland or non-controversial, if it produces scarcely a ripple in an institution's consciousness, then arguably it is not worth undertaking. Evaluation only begins to justify the time and resources invested in it if it questions, or provides the basis for questioning, existing practices and orthodoxies, if it provides for a consideration of alternative analyses of and solutions to the problems of teaching and learning. In other words, it is premised on a view of teaching and learning as themselves problematic and of improved professional practice as requiring a climate of critical commitment, leading to what we term the 'theorizing institution'.

Thus there is clearly a paradox in the notions of successful/problematic evaluation. All the evaluation studies we report were 'successful' in that they happened. In this sense the Charlesford and Enlands evaluations stand as notable success stories in a field where many institutions get no further than merely talking about the desirability of evaluation. The most obviously 'successful' studies, however, had in common a relatively smooth passage from inception to dissemination and response; other studies encountered difficulties along the line, usually at the reporting stage. Almost invariably it was the controversial, challenging nature of the reported findings which caused the problems and inasmuch as they disturbed existing assumptions and orthodoxies they could in our terms be counted 'successful'. However, the crux of the matter is the extent to which these difficulties provided the impetus for development; there has to be a resolution of the controversy; there has to be positive response to the challenge. Without this moving beyond the point of dissonance, an evaluation may remain unsuccessful. In practice, among the evaluation studies which are halted at this critical point may be some with the richest potential for enhancing an institution's understanding of its work.

However, there are two further complicating factors in the search for criteria for judging the success of institutional evaluation. One is the perhaps obvious point that it is not institutions but individuals and groups who receive and respond to evaluation studies, who have the capacity to question their work, to generate hypotheses, to identify and solve professional problems. The studies we undertook tended to be reacted to differently by different people. 'Successful' is thus a relative designation in a further respect — by it we infer a favourable response which was widespread rather than limited to a few. The 'problematic' evaluations, by the same token, were successful and useful for at least a proportion of staff but the scale of adverse response (whether defined numerically or in terms of institutional power) was such as to prevent substantial movement beyond the point of challenge at the whole institutional level.

The other complicating factor is the necessity of using short-term criteria for evaluating evaluation. Ideally, institutions develop unimpeded over a substantial period of time, and the impact of a major innovation like a new course or an evaluation programme ought not to be judged too soon. But the contraction of teacher education in the late 1970s, which has now spread to the rest of higher education and to the schools, has had the effect of telescoping time-scales and making institutions very present-time oriented: one year's development plan is next year's waste paper. The future is something we come to dread rather than plan for confidently, and an innovation worth the effort of development is one which delivers the goods now rather than in five years' time. The most apposite model of educational change in the 1980s should perhaps be grounded in catastrophe theory rather than evolutionary theory. Thus it could well be that in the longer term our 'problematic' studies were or may prove to be, for some people, highly successful in terms of individual/institutional growth, and in any event we think it likely that something of individual professional or institutional advantage was gained from every one of our studies, wherever those that so gained may now be, and however we are forced to judge the studies in these chapters.

Conclusion

In this opening chapter we have attempted to convey something of the practical and conceptual ramifications acquired by the portmanteau term 'evaluation' once it is applied to the day-to-day practices of educational institutions. We have also set out some of the terms, ideas and frameworks we shall use later — and which we invite readers to test — in analysing our experiences as evaluation practitioners and in drawing on these experiences to devise general principles for the conduct of institutional evaluation in a variety of settings. We turn now to the practice of evaluation in two institutions, Enlands and Charlesford colleges.

Note

1 This externalization of accountability issues is comparable to what we have identified as a problem in relation to the basic concept of 'evaluation'. It would be interesting to speculate on why this has happened. Perhaps it reflects a tradition in educational research of looking in everybody's backyard but one's own. Or perhaps it reflects the reality of the institutions (universities) in which many of the leading writers on these issues work and which are notable for their lack of attention to formal educational evaluation other than student assessment and for their neglect of internal accountability questions.

2 ENLANDS AND CHARLESFORD: CONTEXTS FOR EVALUATION IN PRACTICE

The raw material for much of this book's analysis is our experience as agents in two independently conceived and conducted attempts to foster institutional self-evaluation. These took place in institutions which had sufficient in common for a contrast between the approaches to evaluation to be instructive: both were large, confident, respected and — by their own lights — progressive colleges of education; both sought to capitalize on the opportunities provided by the James Report (DES, 1972a) and to develop new courses in conjunction with a move from university to CNAA validation.

Ten years later the institutions' circumstances could not be more different. The one we call 'Enlands' is now one of the new colleges of higher education but its story has been nevertheless one of evolution and continuity. 'Charlesford', following the drastic pruning of teacher education in the mid-seventies, and by an accident of geography typical of the way teacher education was 're-organized' during that period (Hencke, 1978; Harding, 1978, and 1979), has dwindled from a large free-standing institution to a mere fragment of one of Britain's largest polytechnics.

We see these contexts, of expansion and relative stability followed by rapid change, as encompassing experiences representative not only of most teacher-education institutions in the mid-seventies but also of many schools, polytechnics, colleges and universities in the eighties. Yet at the same time institutional self-evaluation is by definition an activity whose character is unique to each institution, so that while general issues and principles can be extracted from two institutions' experiences to guide policy and practice in others, the actual decisions in every case must also be embedded in close analysis of institutional particularities.

Similarly, for an outsider to make his own sense of the processes we report and discuss in this book and for him to have some means of testing the validity of the analyses, principles and conclusions we put forward, he needs some background or contextual information. This we now provide, concentrating on the history of innovation, management and evaluation at the two colleges.

Enlands College

Growth and change

Enlands was founded in 1964 and was one of the last colleges of education to be built in the United Kingdom. The first principal appointed young staff as part of deliberate policy. Many of these were straight from school teaching rather than from other colleges of education.

When the first students were admitted in 1964, the college was still incomplete. The staff/student ratio was such that most staff were able to teach in a comprehensive school nearby. Perhaps this direct contact with school teaching, the recent experience of the staff and the liberal educational philosophy of the principal, rapidly established the college as an innovative yet firmly grounded institution which extended its influence nationally.

The college offered the three-year Teachers' Certificate validated by the local university, with whom relations were cordial and benign. The programme of study devised by the college required all students, whether primary or secondary, to study a main subject for three years. This emphasis on the academic study of a subject was felt to be important both to indicate to the students their potential for academic study and so they might not be stigmatized, particularly on entering secondary school teaching, as being without the experience of academic study in depth. Study of at least one area in depth was retained as part of the teacher preparation course for all students in later programmes devised by the college.

The college grew in size. The staff were innovative in the school curriculum as well as in their own subjects within higher education. When staff left, and this was infrequent, many moved on to university or school inspectorate appointments. The first principal was appointed to a university chair in education in 1968.

The new principal held to a similar line on institutional management, staff appointment and encouragement of innovative activities. It was evident in his new appointments that he had an interest in promoting a social science perspective on educational theory. The innovative endeavours addressed their message and product more and more to an external audience. The young staff had developed their ideas, written their books and papers, developed their curriculum materials, explored the implementation of ideas and were now prepared and confident to address a wider audience under, for example, the auspices of the Department of Education and Science, the British Council and the Schools Council. Entrepreneurship was encouraged and rewarded.

The university had agreed that selected students, on successful completion of a fourth year, be awarded the Bachelor of Education degree. The fourth year consisted of further study of the academic subject plus educational studies, rather than advanced professional preparation. Validation of the degree acknowledged the academic capabilities of the staff. The college had grown, partly by a somewhat tense inclusion of a smaller but longer-established college of education.

Responsibility for teaching, assessment, administration and entrepreneurship rested within departments, each with its own head. The heads of departments were predominantly those that had been appointed by the first principal within the first three years of his incumbency. The college expanded its reputation as an innovative place but to this was added the image of thrust and competitiveness. In the national context of teacher preparation the college stood out as fresh thinking, as experimental and as capable of turning out teachers sought after by schools.

With all these institutional qualities the principal was, not unexpectedly, appointed as a member of the committee under Lord James commissioned to inquire into the preparation of teachers. The principal had been engaged in this debate for several years, his articles appearing in various journals. He was the sole representative of the colleges of education on the committee. He was politically astute at all levels and, along with surprisingly few other principals of colleges of education, quickly realized that prompt planning for diversified programmes of study would be required by the college to maintain its size and staff.

This planning began in 1973, its urgency underlined by the December 1972 White Paper *Education: A Framework for Expansion* which indicated that the colleges of education would face considerable reduction in their teacher preparation student numbers (DES, 1972b). The planning was set about with gusto.

The college was already considering unit-based course arrangements before the DES circular 6/74 suggested that a unit-based course arrangement, for a college of between 500–1500 students (Enlands by now had 1300), might be an effective structural means for building diversified programmes of study. A four-year B.Ed. honours degree was devised on a linked-course unit basis. A three-year B.A. was planned to share many of the first- and second-year B.Ed. units.

The college was reorganized. A middle level of management was introduced to deal with the incipient B.A. and B.Ed., and with in-service courses and professional studies. This was a first attempt to construct a 'matrix' organization in the college, one axis defining programme management responsibilities, the other course and teaching responsibilities. As part of the reorganization the head of department position disappeared, freeing some staff, particularly junior members, to devise their own courses of study for inclusion in the B.A. and B.Ed. This freeing for some staff was cause for elation and a stimulus to further creative course-design.

The B.A./B.Ed. with a two-year Diploma in Higher Education as envisaged in the James Report, all sharing from the pool of course units, was not an acceptable innovation to the local university. The Council for National Academic Awards, which had up to that time dealt almost exclusively with polytechnics and colleges of art, was approached to be the validating body. The congenial, benign relationship with the local university shifted into a tough, questioning, seemingly unsympathetic relationship with the CNAA.

In 1973, a unit-based B.Ed. was validated by the CNAA. Not all the units and courses proposed were approved. The matrix organization did not emerge on this occasion: the hierarchical organization continued.

In November 1974, the college's party visiting the CNAA, which consisted of middle level management, principal and deputy principal, met a rejection of the B.A. and Dip.H.E. proposals. This rejection was a shock to the college as a whole. Some staff regretted the move from university validation. The senior management, who had been largely instrumental in the college's successful innovation in the past, had met its most difficult obstacle. The scheme had not met the 'rigorous' standards of the CNAA. The B.A. was not considered by the CNAA to have qualities that were markedly distinct from the B.Ed. The CNAA was viewed as 'polytechnic dominated' and thus unable to judge the qualities of the diversified package in their concern about potential competition for students. Certainly, the CNAA was only just becoming familiar with the colleges of education and was unfamiliar with unit-based programmes of study.

Mark Two of the Dip.H.E./B.A. was submitted in 1975. In July 1975 the CNAA visited the college. The meeting was described by one senior manager as 'hysterical', full of confusion and misunderstanding. The Dip.H.E. was accepted with links to the B.Ed., although the Dip.H.E. had been planned to lead into the B.Sc. or the B.A. The B.A., still based on a course-unit arrangement, was rejected for a second time. The first group of students registered for the Diploma in Higher Education in 1975.

These two rebuffs quelled the college's elation. The creative inspiration, energy and enthusiasm were now tempered by 'hard-headed' management concerns such as with logistics, resources and administration. These were qualities that the CNAA experience had fostered in the college. The CNAA's influence on the validation of the diversified programmes marked a period of change in the college. What followed was adjustment.

The B.A. (Mark Three) with a conventional Major/Minor programme structure was approved in 1976. Four Majors were acceptable to the CNAA. More Majors were planned. The subject departments were resuscitated, although a programme director and committee oversaw the whole degree to ensure that each Major was working within the aims of the programme as a whole.

The areas of entrepreneurship had shrunk. However, in-service provision for teachers was an expanding area with a wide net. Educational management courses became prominent. The college had validated its first Master's degree, in School Administration. The principal, who had been deeply involved in the changes, left for an international post in 1978.

The college was in a state of uncertainty. Medium-term aims could not be well defined as decisions about the future of the public sector of higher education and the colleges of education in particular were still being made by the DES and LEAs. The plans for a revised B.Ed. and Dip.H.E., emerging from working parties which had met for eighteen months, were not taken up by the college. The working party on academic structure, the last to be convened, supplanted the 'who would do what on the B.Ed. and Dip.H.E.' working party schemes. The matrix organization re-appeared and was approved by the academic board. A new level of responsibility, for courses and teaching and internal appointments, was made just before the second principal left. One of the middle managers had left, leaving four in post. These became the directors of the four programmes. The college's anomalous relationship to the formal guidelines of the Burnham salary structure was largely rectified. To some extent the previous levelling out of salary scales had precluded a separation of the management functions from teaching with what some considered fruitful consequences for innovation and cohesion. Now for the most part this separation was extant.

In September 1978, the new principal joined the college. He was not the recipient of a gift but the inheritor of a legacy. To the uncertainty of aims with its consequences for leadership had been added an acrimony amongst long-serving colleagues provoked by the recent internal appointments.

The new principal took a rational/consultative approach to the college's problems, appealing to intellect through debate. Staff who had tended to be publicly quiescent emerged as influential in these debates about the future of the college. Curriculum development and the nature of the student constituency became priority topics for debate.

To allow for the new expertise and knowledge envisaged in the curriculum development more than a dozen staff became voluntarily redundant. Research in a broad sense was promoted as an activity of worth. The rational planning, for which the principal received widespread support, eventually came to a point at which staff had to be designated to take responsibility for the development of curriculum in different areas. The principal commissioned established senior managers to instigate these developments, perhaps because they had written papers that indicated that they had thought deeply about the college's dilemmas. In fact, these papers were, for the most part, emulative and synthetic. Staff influential in the debates withdrew their active support from the appointed developers. To this unspoken vote of 'no confidence' was added, after the failure of the planned programmes to gain approval by the CNAA, the voice of the principal.

In 1980 a scheme design group and a scheme evaluation group were established to devise a revised B.Ed. based on a previous B.Ed. programme. This process of design and evaluation was searching and consultative, and was successful in that the revised B.Ed. was validated in June 1981.

Further planning ensued whilst the college developed and diversified in the areas of new programmes, courses and research. Diversification for expansion, came to an end with the 'capping of the pool' (1980), the ending of the funding which enabled colleges to increase their student numbers outside the restrictions of those specified by their intial teacher-training quota. The final set of new appointments was made and the college's future development was to be defined, largely, by internal initiative.

The development of evaluative research

The idea for an evaluative research project emerged in 1973, during the expansionist period. Negotiations with the DES committed the college to carrying out the research but by the time the project received funds in late 1975, the college's confidence had been shaken, mainly by the CNAA experience. The management no longer wished for the detail of the case study or the approach of illuminative evaluation. These approaches would show in detail the problems the college faced in its adjustments. The study of institutional change was to become incidental to the study of student choice. The project title, the senior research fellow suggested, should be revised to read 'A Study of Institutional Change in the Context of Student Choice'. The wit was not appreciated.

In the research proposal, institutional self-study was proposed as being useful for development in the expected circumstances of institutional stability. Yet, to be responsive, self-study and evaluation should emerge from issues, concerns, problems and successes of practitioners. The information in the research brief did not address problems of the staff in general, but more the problems and issues encountered by senior staff engaged in forward planning and policy decisions.

One of the researchers' initial problems was to identify an appropriate audience for their reports. Although each college gave responsibility for liaison with the research project to a senior member of staff, these 'link-men' did not have a clear mandate to make independent decisions regarding dissemination of the project's reports. It seemed to the researchers that if the only people to receive their reports would be those suggested by the link-men, then reports dealing with sensitive issues in the areas of policy and programme might have a circulation too limited to further attempts to encourage self-study.

The two-page description of the project and its intentions which follows was distributed to senior and other key staff. An invitation that further copies would be available for them to distribute to subordinate staff was not taken up. The researchers decided instead to make their own distribution of the document to all staff about two months later. Once again, there was no response.

☐ *A study of student choice in the context of institutional change*

The project is funded by the Department of Education and Science from March 1976 to September 1979. Although the project team will be based at this college, complementary information will be collected from two other colleges.[1]

Mr Clem Adelman (senior research fellow), Mr Ian Gibbs (research associate) and a secretary comprise the funded team.

A steering committee of staff from the three colleges, together with university and DES representatives, will advise the evaluation team and in turn will receive particular reports.

A context for the project

Higher education in the United Kingdom is undergoing both radical reorganization and reorientation. Corporate and individual identities are being lost and reconstructed. Tertiary educational establishments are competing for declining numbers of prospective students. Universities, polytechnics, colleges of higher education (those with less than 75 per cent of teacher-education courses) and colleges of education are endeavouring to offer distinctive courses and facilities. The three colleges involved in this project offer the student a choice of main options and of supplementary and complementary units. The student is thus responsible, to some extent, for the construction of the curriculum he will follow. Successful completion of units within courses contributes to B.Ed., B.A. and Dip.H.E. qualifications.

One of the project's main tasks will be to investigate the effects of student choice, within and across courses, on the academic schedules, staff and student organizations etc. The capability of the colleges to deal with the effects of the student choice will be monitored. The internal and external constraints and freedoms impinging on the students' abilities to construct their own curriculum will also be under surveillance. The levels of student and staff satisfaction and frustration with the courses will be assessed over time. It is hoped that the many layers of different freedoms and constraints will show patterning over time. For instance, the 'stress points' of organizations will probably be multi-contributory rather than simple linear peaks.

Evaluation reports will be sent to various audiences within the college. It is hoped that people will respond to these reports and that the evaluators will be able to monitor these responses both directly and indirectly. Through sustained cyclic feedback, the college members and organizations may become self-critical and more capable of situating their decision-making in the context of the welfare of the whole college. The overriding aim of the study will be to evaluate the processes which contribute to the reconsideration and revitalization of courses, to staff self-esteem and the concomitant structural re-arrangements.

Methodology

We will conduct a 'responsive evaluation' (Stake, 1975). We will be independent evaluators neither attached nor allied to any factions. We want to be plainly seen as fair-minded, taking into account all points of view. The information we collect will be handled with care. Confidential matters will be cleared with informants before being allowed wider circulation in reports.

A group of about forty students (about 10 per cent of the total 1976 intake) will be studied for two, maybe three years. They will be interviewed whilst still prospective students and, hopefully, will be willing to keep notes and be interviewed about their academic college experiences.

From this longitudinal group (which will have smaller equivalents in the other two colleges) the evaluators will derive many student viewpoints. Questionnaires to the whole of the 1976 intake will be based upon the more extensive information from the longitudinal group. Discrepancies between the students' accounts and those of the staff will be pursued. The evaluation will involve both fieldwork and statistical procedures — hopefully one will shed light on the other.

Clem Adelman
Ian Gibbs

12 May 1976   □

Testing the water — the induction reports

In order to register the presence of the project and to give an indication of the range of work it would engage in, a portrayal of the induction of new students at each of the three colleges, along with tabulated results of a questionnaire they had completed on entry, were distributed to staff. A note inviting comment and response was appended. By portraying the events which had taken place the report to each college was intended to reflect their approach to the task of induction and, in particular, how institutional values and aims were embodied in the addresses of staff to the new students. As an indication of the style, an extract follows. Pseudonyms replace real names.

☐ *7 P.M. WEDNESDAY, 22 SEPTEMBER*

The resident freshers that arrive to hear the principal's welcome look transformed from the wet, bedraggled afternoon crowd. Many are formally dressed in casual clothes. Clean blue jeans, impeccably placed head-scarves — North American style.

The principal, in a beige suit, enters by the side door followed by Mary Lee and Mike Goodman. The head porter who holds open the door is acknowledged by the Principal with a word and a smile. Hush as the principal ascends the platform around which bouquets of flowers are aesthetically distributed.

'The front two rows are empty,' the principal says, seemingly drawing on his experience of analogous social situations in schools. 'It's not punishment to come to the front.' Many students move, yet the front row remains deficient. There are about two hundred in the hall.

The head porter sits down. We are ready to begin.

The principal expresses his concern that some of last year's students did not seem to know him. He compares being a resident to being in lodgings. 'Being a resident is important — a major difference. Certain features are similar to home, the food may not be as good, the room is different.' A girl coughs loudly for the fourth time. He suggests, 'You could do with my glass of water.' The students are amused.

'There are well accepted conventions of behaviour in lodgings, you are grown up. . . . You have one year guaranteed residence, maybe two years. Most of you who opted for first-year residence have been able to do so. . . . Establish friendships. . . . The staff will be interested in your residential life.'

The principal talks about possible homesickness, especially if students are in lodgings. He forewarns that the time between the end of lectures and the evening meal can be a strain.

'The freedom of the individual is only possible if there is respect for others in their social and private lives.'

'Enlands is your place, the college takes life because of your presence. The quality of life is very much what you make it. You are in charge until the rest of the students arrive.'

The third-year students, although in residence, are out in schools on their teaching practice whilst the hosts — about 10 per cent of the second years — are mainly in lodgings.

'We do not prescribe activities but we hope you will take up opportunities. You might begin to feel stoned out of your minds about the number of things going on.'

'You'll find like most people who come to the college, like those at a recent Council of Europe Conference say, how marvellous the non-tutorial staff are . . . the porters, kitchen staff, cleaners.'

'You're here for a rather long conference' (referring to their courses of study).

'Facilities for the non-resident and lodging students are not as marvellous as we would like . . . team up with residents.'

'We don't have a very formal structure. Most people will respond. Don't only use the 'blue' book (the *Handbook*) — ask anyone.'

(A widespread problem for freshers during the first two weeks was what and where were the pigeon holes!)

The principal introduces Mary Lee, the senior tutor, whose role includes that of the general welfare of the students. She tells the freshers that the host students will attend to important things; tutors to minor things, in general, in the beginning. 'The host students are second-years. Third-year students are those sharing the hostels with the first-years.' Mary Lee concludes, asking whether the student union president is present. The head porter goes to fetch her.

The principal, Mary Lee and Mike Goodman leave by the side door. The student union president and the student union executive have not yet arrived. This will be their first appearance in front of the freshers. The side door is still open as the student union executive arrive, led by the student union president, followed by two girls each with a half-pint glass and three males, one of whom, whilst re-arranging the seating, collides with the flower arrangements. The student union president introduces the executive saying that they will only deal with routine matters. ☐

Response to the induction report

The response to the induction report at Enlands ranged from 'A witty piece of writing', 'Just as I see the event', 'Very nice, very funny, but I ask myself, "Is it research?"'. Other members of staff turned back some extracts from the report to apply to the researchers ('Mr Adelman, wearing a pigeon blue jacket') or asserted that some of the brief observations reported were not typical of the activities of the particular groups involved. In the latter case further details of antecedent and subsequent events around those described in the report were provided by the respondents. The main thrust of the critical comments was about the non-typicality of some of the events of that particular year. For instance, the display of complementary courses was held to have been somewhat chaotic because the larger space in which it was usually held was unavailable.

The induction reports were intended to serve not only the purposes of reporting but also of making some sort of substantive announcement of the work of the project. Although the number of responses was few, the description of the induction, which included transcripts of the people involved as well as a list of points for discussion by the college, was expected to make some impact, as it reflected the practices of the college. The induction report, as was made explicit in the text, was based on observations and, to an extent, on some interpretations by the researchers. To provide a foretaste of the conventional work that the project would also engage in, results from the student entry questionnaire were provided at the same time.

The researchers realized that the responses of individual staff would reflect particular interests and vulnerabilities. The project required more extensive institutional responses arising from public discussions amongst staff. The researchers' reticence to interpret was based on esoteric values of 'disinterested' research, whereas members of the institution were only able to respond (given their other obligations) when provided with explicit texts related to their practices. The apparent social relationships within the institution were such that, from what was included in the induction report, little or no loss of face in the eyes of any other members was felt. The induction report did not receive reflective comments from staff about the values of the institution and the appropriateness of the content and format of the induction.

The induction reports, in a limited way, did have one desired consequence of establishing an identity for the researchers as persons independent of rather than co-opted into the institutional authority relationships.

The Enlands induction report was not a complete account of what was observed and recorded. This was known to some sections of the college who had attended the induction and witnessed many of the events that were reported. A particular address by a senior member of staff was summarized rather than detailed or provided in transcript. By any standards, this address misrepresented colleagues, was inaccurate and was misleading to students engaged in confirming their initial choice of courses. The staff who had witnessed the address requested that the Senior Research Fellow include the transcript in the induction report. Separately, the person who had made the address requested that no transcript be included.

Although evaluators may try to present 'disinterested' descriptions of events, they have little control of how this information might be used. It was not an aspiration of the project to stir personal animosities or to foster character assassination, rather, goodwill within the institution had to be developed by the researchers in order to retain access to staff and foster institutional self-study. The researchers did not consider that fostering goodwill meant that the researchers would defer to the status quo. They wished to address controversial issues but, in order to recognize these, they needed to be accepted into the confidence of the institution's staff. However, even at the time of the release of the induction report, the researchers had only a limited awareness of institutional norms and history. The contentious address could not be set in relation to normal practice. The decision to provide a brief summary of the address was, from the point of view of the independence/non-sectional status of the researchers, justified.

The questionnaire results were sent out in tabulated form broken down into male/female and mature/straight-from-school. A note to the recipient requested suggestions for cross-tabulations. This request was premised on the assumption that practitioners within the college would have most knowledge about which of the results were relevant and could most fruitfully be cross-tabulated. It was also believed that if institutional self-study were to be fostered the staff should have the opportunity to emphasize and raise issues in conjunction with the researchers. No suggestions for cross-tabulations or any other written replies were received from the three colleges. Verbal comments from some of the staff who had received the questionnaires suggested that they were of interest, but that the pressures of other work precluded response. One member of staff, on being asked why she had not replied earlier and in writing, said, 'Why should I be the first to stick my neck out so that you can quote me as an example of response?' This response was echoed by other staff subsequently. Eventually the researchers were forced to make their own interpretation in order to report the substance of the aggregated results to the steering committee.

Developing procedures for the conduct of the project

The response to the induction reports contributed to the researchers' awareness that institutional self-study was an aspect of the research that required major establishment rather than, as we had assumed from the research proposals, consolidation. However, prior to the distribution of the questionnaire and observation of the inductions, some of the problems that might arise within the study had been envisaged. Here is an extract from a document written at the end of June 1976 addressed to staff in the three colleges. The document was to expand the idea of 'responsive' evaluation and to expand the 'philosophy' of the methodology of the project.

☐ We consider that the experience of participants, within the institutions, should be collected in order to locate issues and themes that are live and relevant. Whatever the rhetoric surrounding the introduction of any innovation, actual practice has unexpected, unintended aspects. This responsive evaluation seeks to discover and explore the gaps between rhetoric, aspiration and practice. But, having located discrepancies we do not wish to be seen to be making judgements. We wish to remain apart from policy and decision-making within the colleges. Any influence we might have would be through our reports, and their discretionary distribution. The evaluators, having a non-judgemental and non-aligned stance in relation to the participants in the affairs of the institution, should be able to collect honest accounts from all participants within the organization. The evaluators' reports then, should encompass, in a fair way, many sides of any issue (multiple realities). No other persons in the organization are so free, and untainted by the networks of power and control.

However, only by understanding the formal and informal organization structures which control and exert power can the evaluators become discerning about whom should be recipients of reports. We do not want to upset or shock, both of which can be the result of indiscriminate blanket distribution of any report. We prefer reports to go in the first instance to those who are in a position to act on them, modifying their practices, if they judge them unsatisfactory in the light of the report. We take it that a person who has been interviewed should have a transcript of the interview, not only for the purposes of reflection and, perhaps, action, but also to engender his control over the data. We would avoid contributing to any conflicts arising from personal vindictiveness, or mistakes, but would contribute to debates arising from what seem to be structural/communication inadequacies, lack of awareness of the gap between ideal and actual, secret and unjust use of power. To repeat, the reports would be from as many points of view as possible.   □

However, the researchers did not realise that distribution of and response to documents would be so problematic. Their aspirations, as set out in this June 1976 document, proved difficult to fulfil.

The sectional nature of the responses to the induction report, the lack of response to the tabulated questionnaire, along with the decision of the researchers to decide their own distribution of documents, neither fostered institutional self-study nor the independence of the researchers. The false equation of institutional self-study with the deliberate, yet invited collaboration of action research was realized and the responsibility for distribution of documents was shifted to the discussion groups within the college.

Although intervention in the workings of the college by suggesting that particular groups of staff come together to discuss project documents and respond to these could be plausibly negotiated in action research, in fact, the researchers were to become the respondents to initiatives suggested by the colleges. The opportunity to set up discussion groups, which would mediate the work of the project into the institutional activities, arose as a response to a suggestion at the project steering committee meeting by the principal of Le Gume. He made it clear to the steering committee that he was concerned, after the release of the induction report, about the work of the project and its effects on his college staff and asserted that in future all documents would be looked at by a working party which his college would set up. The researchers made it clear to the steering committee that they would welcome such discussion groups in the three colleges. The suggestion to set up the discussion groups was made in 1977. Copies of this note were sent to the link-men in the three colleges for distribution to those staff who might be interested or appointed to serve as members of the discussion group.

□ Would the discussion group be willing to consider documents arising from the project, suggesting amendments, emphases and distribution? . . .

Documents arising from the project's work in each of the colleges are initially sent to the 'link-man', who makes the decision as to whether these documents are amenable for presentation to the college discussion group. During the discussions the research team will be in attendance in order to supply required additional evidence and to support their writings by reasoned argument. The discussion group would make decisions relating to any further distribution of project documents. The discussion group would also suggest amendments to the documents; priorities for investigation; emphases; and modes of presentation and expression that might assist communication. By freeing the research team from the responsibility of distribution the discussion group would allow the researchers to remain independent in this respect. Neither the research team nor the discussion group may be held to be accountable for the effects of the release of such information.

If the discussion group considers that it is able to co-operate with the research team in these respects, feedback from the project will be greatly facilitated.   □

Although membership of the discussion group depended on the extent to which institutions controlled the flow of information in a hierarchical manner, these discussion groups did fulfil the requirements of taking on the responsibility for distribution of project documents, having responded to these documents either in writing or in the presence of the researchers.

The researchers, having realized the perils of intervention in the communication channels of the institutions, quickly reiterated their independence as evaluators; independence meaning that the evaluators were open to discussions with any individual or groups within the institutions and would direct their work or reports to any group, rather than directly or apparently serve any particular set of interests.

In order to achieve this independence, the researchers required 'knowledgeable users' (Adelman, 1981b) who could respond to the reports. Having failed to get each college to respond as a community of knowledgeable users, the project faced the task of creating such groups: groups to which the reports which would be released in the first instance rather than simply following established institutional communication channels. The research team's original aspiration — to promote a 'responsive' evaluation — could still be upheld in a modified form in relation to these discussion groups rather than in relation to the whole institution.

Responses to the research reports

Only twelve staff across the three colleges commented on the project's early reports. As researchers, we had made the assumption that information which arose directly from the college work would be sought by staff. Given the college's turbulent present and uncertain future, these reports, the researchers thought, would be welcomed by staff at the very least as 'indications' of how the colleges were adjusting to the diversification of courses. However, many staff were so deeply engaged in planning new courses or sometimes maintaining continuity of present courses, that they could only attend to those aspects of the institution's plans that impinged on their own circumstances. The few staff that responded to the researcher's reports were those who were able, either through their senior position as managers or by their ability to go beyond their own circumstances, to think about the institution as a whole.

As the succession of 'bad news' from the Department of Education and Science and the LEAs hit the colleges, the attention of staff turned more to newspapers and weekly journals; to leaked reports as well as official DES and LEA announcements.

These sources of information were used to feed speculation about where the next 'cuts' would occur and particularly whether their college would be the 'victim'. Institutional planning became a matter of how to preserve present resources and attract students. A DES point of view of these years indicates the prolonged uncertainty. 'Our nightmare was that the operation [of facilitating closure of colleges] might become a long-drawn-out shambles. The institutions concerned were not the Department's direct responsibility and we had no powers except to require the discontinuation of teacher training. In February 1973 we hoped to reach final decisions by the end of 1974. Despite two general elections and changes of ministers, by mid-1975 much more extensive contraction and reorganization was operating than had been envisaged in the 1972 White Paper. Only the continuing fall in the birth rate required the final phase of 1976–7.' (Harding, 1979).

This attempt to foster institutional self-study and evaluation through feedback to research reports and responsive evaluation was apparently unsuccessful for at least the first year of the project. In retrospect, the researchers' assumption that staff would read the reports and communicate their comments was naïve, yet such a rational model of research and development is widespread in theory if not in practice.

As the researchers were employed on a contract, they had to take at face value, at least initially, the assurance of the co-operation and interest of the staff in the colleges. However, their initial 'tests of the water' indicated otherwise. Unlike the Charlesford case, the crucial work of negotiating an evaluation constitution within each of the three colleges, to identify audiences and define procedures for commissioning evaluation and reporting, was lacking in this contract research-based project.

The establishing of the discussion groups was an opportunity to secure such a place in the college's life. But the discussion groups were not elected, neither had they any representation within the formal decision-making committees and boards within the colleges. Interpretations and comments expressed in the group did, however, eventually contribute to the dissemination, within the colleges, of parts of the project's reports that were considered particularly pertinent to debates. An extract from one of the evaluations of the work of the project (requested by the researchers, written by the 'link-man' towards the end of the project and included in the final report to the DES), attests to the time that elapsed before the project's pertinence was appreciated.

☐ A discussion group comprising a cross section of staff ('senior' and 'junior') was established to consider these papers, but pressure of other meetings on the time available to the group made it possible to give only modest consideration to these interim statements. The college, as a whole, found it very difficult to discuss and to respond to these statements. It was not always clear whether the interim statements were primarily intended to be helpful and useful to the college or to stimulate discussion that would provide feedback to the research study. Staff had difficulty in discerning what feedback the researchers were hoping for from this exercise, and the college regrets any inadequacies on its part in providing feedback to the research team. With hindsight, it is now recognized that the researchers possessed much more information than was apparent during the discussion of the interim statements. However, at the time, staff often felt that these brief statements were not based on a true understanding of the complexity of the college programme and, at worst, were naïve. Whether this can be attributed to a mismatch of perceptions or to a distorted view of reality held by the college staff remains a matter for speculation.

Seen in the context of the final report these interim statements now have an interest and significance which was not apparent on their original publication. Although the college was not able to utilize effectively the interim information in its official deliberations, the final report will undoubtedly contribute significantly to future discussions. The fact that many of the findings have confirmed the beliefs held by those involved in taking the original decisions that led to a diversified programme lends support to the professional judgement of those staff. The concerns which have emerged independently in the college and in the study, and to which some clear answers are now available, are a validation of the relevance of the study and signal the importance of self-evaluation in considering the effectiveness of its on-going programmes. □

Charlesford College

The evolution of a college culture

In its heyday — the late sixties and early seventies — Charlesford college was, with up to 1650 male and female students and 150 academic staff, one of the largest and best respected colleges of education in the country. Prior to 1974 it offered two teacher-training courses, a B.Ed. and a Postgraduate Certificate in Education, with annual intakes of about 500 and 150 students respectively. Both courses were validated by the local university, and both were in the mainstream style of the period: the B.Ed. had the usual main/subsidiary 'academic' subjects plus education theory, practical 'curriculum' subject studies and teaching practice, and it trained students for all school age ranges. The PGCE combined education theory with teaching subject 'method' courses in the standard three-term course-work/teaching practice/coursework sandwich.

The college was located in an attractive suburb of a large northern industrial city. Physically it combined the elegance of the late eighteenth-century country house at its core with an accretion of undistinguished but sympathetically planned and sited teaching blocks, purpose-built to meet the massive expansion of the 1960s (the college had been founded as an emergency training college in 1946). Teaching and tutorial conditions were good and the institution provided an eminently congenial physical environment in which to work.

The college had three principals from its foundation in 1946 to the completion of the merger with the city's polytechnic in 1977. The leadership style of each was very different and had a considerable influence on the way the college's capacity for innovation developed and on the very varied responses which different sorts of innovation provoked among staff. The first principal exercised traditional authority and the college structure was strictly hierarchical. Loyalty to the institution and deference to rank were emphasized, and consensus was assumed. For most of this period the college was a small and fairly intimate establishment, so that while both staff and students were expected to know their place, life had a quality which was lost once the institution expanded in the mid-1960s.

The second principal was totally different. To him the most valued institutional qualities were change, ambition and intellectual liveliness. The rapid expansion of the 1960s was seen as an opportunity to develop on the fringes of the city a sizeable centre of academic excellence, one which might even rival the city-centre university. During his three-year tenure the college developed a considerable academic reputation and the level of qualification of the staff appointed during this period and subsequently was on the whole markedly higher than in many other colleges of education. The seeds of the innovativeness which characterized the college's later work were sown during this period even though it was only after the second principal left that they bore fruit in the form of four new teacher-education courses, including the first Initial B.Ed. in England to be validated by the Council for National Academic Awards.

The other contribution of the second principal, and one which had a notable impact on subsequent development, was the promotion of what he termed 'creative conflict'. In practice this meant that the old order of relative stability premissed on a traditional, almost feudal authority structure, was replaced by a period during which staff with ideas, energy and (especially) political *savoir-faire* were encouraged to break out of the constraints of formal hierarchy to seek to further their individual ambitions, provided that these were consistent with the principal's vision of the institution as a centre of excellence.

The college's third (and last) principal, appointed in 1970, inherited this newer tradition. He was appointed, it was generally thought at the time, on the assumption that he would promote stability rather than conflict, and especially would not follow his predecessor in engaging in protracted and public battles with the local authority. Yet under him the energies fostered in the previous three years were channelled into major and radical curricular and organizational innovations. For his lack of personal dynamism and his disinclination to exercise the sort of charismatic leadership demonstrated previously provided the necessary vacuum for politicized staff to realize their ambitions and for major shifts in the distribution of power as between groups and individuals.

Under this third principal, once the new courses were established, the key figures and groups whose emergence was facilitated by the climate and norms established by his predecessor were able to consolidate their power, and the institution settled uneasily into a new structure (which in its way, as we shall see, was as rigid and as unable to respond to or initiate genuine innovation as the old simple departmental structure established under the first principal).

Although superficially the college culture had shifted in accordance with changes in leadership styles, there were in fact several fairly distinct value systems or sub-cultures evident at the time the evaluation programme started. For in 1974 there were many staff in the college who had been appointed before 1966 by the first principal, and loyalty to (or nostalgia for) the ideas and order he represented was in some quarters very strong. So too, elsewhere, was commitment to the intellectual vitality and political activism encouraged by his successor. The college in the 1970s was a pluralist institution, and sometimes cultures, traditions and allegiances came into conflict. One notable example was the conflict between the departments, the traditional home of academic authority, and the course committees which were set up to 'manage' the new CNAA degrees, many of whose members were from the political entrepreneurial group identified earlier. These bodies tended to have the impersonal and bureaucratic style of operation encouraged by the third principal's approach to decision-making. They demonstrated fairly clearly that academic vitality and political activism are not necessarily sides of the same coin.

The new courses

The new courses which the evaluation programme was set up to study were, in part, products of the shifts in college climate and power outlined above, but there were two rather more obviously significant causal factors. One was the increasing dissatisfaction in the college, whose academic pride (or, as some thought, conceit) had been nurtured by the second principal, with the extreme paternalism of the local university's validation style and with its reluctance to grant the award of honours for the B.Ed. degrees. The other was the setting up of the Committee of Inquiry under Lord James to investigate teacher training. This committee started work in 1970 and the college was assiduous in its attempts to discover and anticipate the inquiry's likely outcomes (DES, 1972a) and to be seen nationally as a pioneer in the post-James era of teacher education.

As a result of an intensive period of planning which involved a large proportion of the college staff, a new B.Ed. (honours) course was validated by the CNAA in 1973. There followed, fairly quickly, a new PGCE and two in-service B.Ed. courses. The new courses all claimed a degree of radicalism in respect of the familiar conceptual and practical problems of teacher training — the relationship between 'personal' education and 'professional' training, the theory–practice interface, the role and character of school experience, and so on. Much of the impetus for such apparently radical shifts in the conceptual bases of the new courses was provided by relatively junior members of staff who were enabled by the comparative openness and competitiveness of the planning style to gain a hearing for new ideas, provided that these were coherently and persuasively expressed.

The speed of the changes, considering the scale of the innovation and the conceptual shifts embodied in the new courses, was remarkable, and naturally it produced considerable dissonance which, as we shall see, proved to be a major factor in any analysis of both the successes and the failures of the evaluation experiment. Planning on the new B.Ed. started in June 1971. The course was validated in 1973 and took its first students in 1974. Planning started on the PGCE in January 1974 for a June 1975 validation and a September 1975 intake; the two in-service B.Ed.s (which catered for much smaller numbers of students) started in April 1975 and April 1976 respectively after, in each case, a planning period of about one year.

At the start of the evaluation programme, internal government of the college was led by an academic board (set up by the second principal following the publication of the Weaver Report on college government (DES, 1966)), which contained a preponderance of ex-officio senior staff together with some elected staff and student representatives, and supported by a large number of committees. Subsequently, partly as a result of the Houghton salary award which produced the potential anomaly of heads of small departments being paid less than some principal lecturers, and partly in response to the different needs of the new courses, the sixteen small- to medium-sized departments were merged to form five large departments (as indicated in the diagram on page 60) and the committee structure was simplified. Each new course was given a course management committee with course 'officers' responsible under a course leader for the various components. To the now more concentrated departmental structure was added a cross-departmental course management dimension, producing the 'matrix' structure now familiar in this sector of higher education and which also emerged at Enlands. In addition there appeared an executive committee charged with a considerable amount of day-to-day responsibility on behalf of the academic board.

This restructuring produced a greater concentration of power in a relatively small number of hands: there were now five departments, four course committees, an executive committee, a courses committee and one or two other committees of minor significance, and there was substantial overlap in the membership of the major committees. The decision-making power of the academic board became more and more nominal: in fact, one of the recurrent difficulties for both the new courses and the evaluation programme was that while they were all undertaken with full academic board backing, even a unanimous commitment to a particular decision by an ostensibly representative academic board was scarcely a commitment at all in real terms.

Equally significant was the reduction in the power of the departments as a consequence of the appearance of these course management bodies. Departments were now viewed not so much as communities of academics as collections of 'resources' to be drawn on by course managers via their heads (who were designated 'chief resource providers').

Into this arena came the idea of evaluation. The tension inherent in the management/academic matrix was extended to encompass what seem to us to be four recurrent elements in the consciousness of large educational institutions. Firstly, the *management imperative*, represented here by the course committees and the executive committee; secondly, the *academic allegiance* of teaching staff fostered by and focused upon academic departments. Thirdly, the individual teacher's commitment to *professional autonomy*; and fourthly, the *democratic ideal*, (tested here by the style of evaluation adopted), of open appraisal of the institution's collectively-evolved educational activities. These elements represent at first sight paired relations: management/academic allegiance, autonomy/democracy. However, as we shall see later, the tensions are more complex and interpenetrative than this.

The birth of the evaluation idea

The idea, in any educational institution, of undertaking course or curriculum evaluation on any basis beyond what we have termed 'informal' evaluation generally takes some getting used to, and, although curriculum theorists make much of the need for 'formative' as opposed to 'summative' evaluation (Scriven, 1967) more often than not evaluation is tacked on almost as an afterthought. This was the case at Charlesford. However, the roots of the decision to evaluate the four new CNAA-validated courses went back much earlier, to the mid-point in the B.Ed. planning process. A discussion document on the management of innovation proposed the establishment of a 'course development committee' one of whose tasks would be 'to develop a method of, and assist in, course evaluation'. This committee was set up, but the evaluation remit was shelved: the committee had its hands full in steering the extensive programme of course development which was by then under way.

Immediately after the B.Ed. was validated in October 1973 a further discussion document on college management was circulated. This was operationalized in an amended form as a matrix structure of course committees and departments overseen by the executive and course committees to which we referred earlier, and the evaluation commitment reasserted itself in the deliberations of the executive committee the following year. Not preceded by any public discussion of the matter, the committee invited applications from within the college for the post of 'evaluator', in June 1975. The term 'evaluator' carried strong and uncomfortable resonances of inspection and measurement, evident to most members of staff, which were confirmed in the explanatory statements issued by the executive committee and in a paper circulated at about this time which proposed that the evidential basis of course evaluation should be a programme of pre- and post-testing of student attainment in terms of behavioural objectives. It will be recalled that this was the period when Parlett and Hamilton's advocacy (1972) of 'illuminative' evaluation as an alternative to such 'agricultural-botany' models was becoming known beyond the then rather small and inward-looking evaluation community, and MacDonald was developing his analysis of the political dimensions of project evaluations (MacDonald, 1976a). Clearly there was more to course evaluation than testing, and the political challenges of entering what in the UK in 1974 was the virtually uncharted territory of 'internal' institutional self-evaluation were considerable. One of the present authors (Alexander) accepted the post on the conditions that it be redesignated 'adviser on evaluation' and — to quote from the agreed terms of reference — that the initial task should be 'to investigate the possible application to college courses of current and developing approaches to curriculum evaluation and advise the various course committees'. These terms were an attempt to slow the process down to one of development rather than overnight change, to suggest exploration rather than dogma and to make the evaluator by virtue of nomenclature and function a servant rather than a master.

The terms of reference were to be reviewed after one year, when the 'investigation' had been completed. This development year provided a period for pilot evaluation studies on the new B.Ed. course, discussions with course leaders and departmental members, and an analysis of the current state of evaluation as represented by the literature and in a few projects and institutions (several of whose members formed an informal practitioners' network which led to the setting up of *Evaluation Newsletter* (CRITE and SRHE, 1976–   ). In fact, despite the frequent invocation of 'evaluation' in course development discussions, very little course evaluation of a formal variety was taking place at this time in Britain: there was almost no productive case material to draw on apart from the largely inappropriate experiences of Schools Council style project evaluations, and indeed the very conceptual framework of the evaluation literature was (as we believe it still is) dominated by the funded project consultancy evaluator's perspective. The Charlesford evaluation programme was to be the first major 'internal' institutional self-evaluation in British teacher education; it would have to be home-spun and experimental. However, it was soon apparent that the word 'evaluation' could connote a large range of very varied activities underlying which were some considerable questions about epistemology and the politics of accountability. Unless the college had a clear notion of what in concept and practice it wanted 'evaluation' to mean, it could find itself in deep water. For an internal institutional evaluation the college would need a 'constitution', explicating what evaluation was, what it was not, what purpose it was to serve, who it was for, who should control it, who should undertake it, what methods should be used and how it should be organized.

Such a 'constitution' formed the core of the report which was produced at the end of the pilot year. This constitution appeared in two parts. The first was a set of twenty-one 'goals, roles and principles' for the conduct of the evaluation programme. The second was an organizational specification for translating these into action, which dealt in particular with the terms of reference and membership of the body which was to control the evaluation programme.

Some of the items in the 'constitution' were somewhat parochial and are not listed here. The central items, those of most concern for the committees and academic board when they came to debate the proposals, were as follows:

☐ 1 Course evaluation is essential to course improvement, especially in the case of the new approaches to teacher and higher education which this college now offers.

2 Course evaluation is one of our contractual obligations to the CNAA.

3 Course evaluation is incumbent upon the college in view of its

commitment to democratic procedures: we are all accountable to the college, through the academic board, for the conduct of course teaching and course administration.

4 The main goals of evaluation are to promote improved teaching and learning and to provide all participants in courses with information on a wide range of aspects of a course's operation.

This is in marked contrast to the more usual goals of course evaluation as

(a) measurement of the extent to which learning objectives are achieved, and

(b) provision of information for the use of management only.

The course's assessment procedures should deal with (a), while (b) is seen as of limited practical value, open to suspicion of possible misuse, and potentially anti-democratic.

5 These goals require that evaluation be conducted as far as possible by course teachers and learners, rather than by an individual or group, either inside or outside the college, appointed specifically to 'evaluate'.

6 Evaluation is a continuous activity, and a formalized evaluation programme should likewise operate throughout the life of a course.

7 There is a distinction between informal, intuitive evaluation such as any good teacher or teaching team engages in, and formal evaluation having concerns wider than particular classroom contexts and an audience wider than individual teachers. Charlesford's course evaluation programme will, however, aim to promote and build upon informal evaluation as a way of establishing its formal, college-wide procedures.

8 Once evaluation extends beyond the informal and privatized it acquires an inevitable political dimension, can pose a potential threat to the security of the individual teacher, and becomes open to possible abuse by whoever controls it. The particular risk is that evaluation can become a tool of senior management. It is seen as essential to the security of colleagues and the credibility of the programme that the control of course evaluation be vested in the college as a whole via the academic board; policy on evaluation should be recommended and evaluation processes should be interpreted by a properly constituted col-

lege body, independent, as far as possible, from the interests, constraints and pressures of any one group or individual, but at the same time responsive to all.

9 Course evaluation is a developing field and ready-made evaluation 'solutions' are to be treated with caution. In particular, evaluation procedures raise complex and crucial epistemological, ideological and methodological issues which tend to be ignored in much evaluation debate. The college's evaluation programme must therefore be open and experimental, reflecting the diversity of possible approaches, and itself subject to critical appraisal.

10 Absolute judgements are seldom achievable in course evaluation and consensus over relative judgements is rare. It should be accepted from the outset that different individuals and groups will apply different criteria for judgement and draw different conclusions about a course's value and success. Similarly, no one statement of evaluation 'needs' can be expected in a large pluralist college where courses have been planned on a participatory basis and several teachers are involved in the tuition of each student. Such differences in perspectives should be made explicit and should be utilized, not sacrificed in an attempt to achieve outward unanimity. ☐

On the question of control it was argued in the report that the 'properly constituted body' could not be any existing committee, least of all a course committee:

☐ The evaluation body must represent many interests and perspectives — course management is but one of them. This solution (i.e. course committee control) would be contrary to the criterion of independence with responsiveness and would present credibility problems. . . . Evaluation is vital to effective course management, but the two activities are not synonymous. . . . In the early stages of a new course in particular, but subsequently as well, management bodies have a heavy burden of day-to-day administration. To set up an evaluation programme demands a good deal of time spent in debate, often requiring particular sorts of expertise and disposition: neither time nor such expertise and dispositions can be expected to be available on bodies having a highly instrumental administrative function. ☐

The proposed body was to be an 'evaluation committee' having a balanced representation from course management, teaching staff and students together with ex-officio evaluation officers. It would be empowered to recommend an annual evaluation programme, carry it out as approved by the academic board, and report to all concerned on its findings. (Details of memberships and terms of reference as finally agreed are given on pp. 60–1.)

The process of discussing the adviser's evaluation proposals and sending them, with minor modifications, to the academic board for debate and eventual approval *nem. con.*, was relatively straightforward. In fact it was too easy — considering the serious implications of the scale and style of self-study envisaged. There are three possible explanations for this. The first is that the ground was carefully prepared and many of the political pitfalls were anticipated and avoided. The second is that the sentiments expressed in the evaluation constitution were utterly congruent — theoretically at least — with the sort of professional image which the majority of staff in such institutions wished to project. (We shall return to the role of rhetoric in institutional decision-making in chapter five.) The third and perhaps most persuasive reason is that since nothing like this had been tried previously staff could have no way of really knowing what they were in for and the constitution could only be treated as a theoretical statement. In any event the phenomenon of giving what ought to be contentious and fundamental issues an easy passage (and conversely, subjecting trivial matters to close and sustained debate) occurred several times in the college during this period of innovation. It is possible that the academic board can be accused of not learning to distinguish serious from trivial matters until it was too late, for by and large even the question of institutional survival (following the DES and LEA proposals on cutbacks and reorganization) failed to provoke the level of response and action it merited. We suspect that this experience has been mirrored in many institutions introducing or responding to unprecedented ideas and challenges.

However, behind the apparently ready acceptance of the evaluation proposals were individual and corporate responses which, though at the time they were overwhelmed by the consensus-seeking tendencies of the committees, proved highly significant and durable, and the gap between public vote and private response is an important element in the success of innovations like this one.

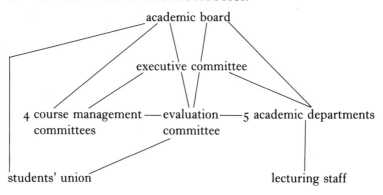

—— indicates formal communication channel and/or representation.

The membership of the evaluation committee as finally established was as follows:

☐ *Ex-officio*

Adviser on evaluation
Evaluation research assistant
(Acting) director of studies
Deputy senior administrative officer

Elected members

1 One from each course committee:
Initial B.Ed.
PGCE
In-service B.Ed.
In-service B.Ed. (Social handicap)
2 One from each college department:
Arts
Science, Mathematics and Physical Education
Humanities and Social Science
Educational Studies
Professional Studies
3 One student from each course:
Initial B.Ed.
PGCE
In-service B.Ed.
In-service B.Ed. (Social Handicap)

The chairman to be elected from other than the *ex-officio* members. ☐

The terms of reference of the evaluation committee were eventually consolidated as follows:

☐ 1 To receive evaluation proposals from:
       course committees
       lecturers
       students;
   2 To formulate annual evaluation programmes for academic board approval;
   3 To implement approved evaluation programmes via course committees, departments and students' union;
   4 To report on each procedure when completed (i) to lecturers immediately concerned, to aid interpretation and report writing; (ii) to course committee concerned, departments and students, via each's representatives; (iii) to academic board;
   5 To promote and report on reaction to studies and action taken as a consequence.   ☐

The new committee started its work at the beginning of the academic year 1975–6 by drawing up a courses evaluation programme for the year which it then implemented in the way we illustrate in chapter 3. This process was repeated annually over a period of four years until the contraction in student numbers, the phasing out of the new courses and the disappearance of Charlesford College following its merger with the local polytechnic (which imposed a very different culture and style of decision-making on the remaining Charlesford staff) made the original 'constitution' both inapplicable and inoperable.

Note

1 These colleges were named in the original documents. They are termed here 'Le Gume' and 'Bellnova'.

3 EVALUATION IN PRACTICE AT CHARLESFORD

Samples from the Charlesford evaluation

We explained in chapter 2 that the Charlesford approach to evaluation rested on a democratic, pluralist ideology which was implemented through a structured and systematized set of procedures. This conjunction of 'open' ideology with in some respects a 'closed' practice might seem paradoxical. Perhaps it is: but our identification of institutional evaluation as a complex decision-making process with political ramifications at every point should serve to explain how this was probably inevitable, especially given the history of the institution. In effect, this is the familiar problem of checks and balances in political institutions: do they enable or do they incapacitate?

This systematization makes the Charlesford approach relatively straight-forward to characterize in terms of the seven evaluation decisions listed in chapter 1. The *institutional framework* for every study was a set procedure laid down in the evaluation committee's terms of reference. An annual programme was drawn up by the committee on the basis of suggestions or bids from the various constituencies — teaching staff, students, course management committees. The agreed version was presented to the academic board as a skeletal statement of issues or *foci*, possibly, but not necessarily including an indication of *methods*. With board approval the committee fleshed out the statement, identified *methods* and *criteria*, with trial stages as appropriate, prepared evaluation instruments (e.g. questionnaires), administered them, analysed data and drafted reports. This central stage in the process was the most variable: clearly a questionnaire to a cohort of students presented wholly different problems from a set of informal and unstructured meetings between college and school staff to discuss students' work in schools. Procedural regularity returned with *dissemination*, though even here the scale produced variety — a single report in one case, a cumulative series of interim reports, each reacted to and modified by clients before the production of a final report, in another. The regularity in dissemination concerned not the scale but the *audience*; all reports were available to all staff and students: those immediately involved received full copies, others received copies of the summaries prepared for the academic board. In addition full reference sets were kept in the college library, the students' union and the staff common-room.

The matter of *application* is more difficult to pin down, and will provide the focus for much of our discussion. Suffice it to say at this stage that the evaluation committee always sought reaction to its reports from the parties concerned, and documented these in a further report for college consumption: clearly it had a strong interest in ensuring that its reports were seen to provoke thought, discussion and, where appropriate, course modification. However, a distinction between 'action' and 'reaction' is critical. Some sort of 'reaction' was taken as obligatory, given that the college as a whole had commissioned the studies. On the other hand, the expectation that every evaluation study should necessarily produce structural changes in courses was seen by the committee as untenable, for an evaluation study provides only one of several possible analyses or viewpoints and in any case its methodology and findings must always be open to challenge on the fundamental epistemological grounds adumbrated in the college's evaluation constitution (items 9 and 10, see page 58), and explored further in chapter 6.

In the interests of avoiding reader confusion, the examples which now follow are all taken from the evaluation of the same course, a degree for intending teachers in primary, secondary and special schools, validated by the CNAA, leading to the award of B.Ed. after three years and B.Ed. (Hons.) after a further year. This was the largest course at Charlesford in terms of students and staff (it started with a student entry of 340 per year), and was the first of the four new courses to be validated by the CNAA. It represented, then, the institution's main collective preoccupation, and although different problems and possibilities for evaluation arose on the other three courses, most were also encountered on the B.Ed. The examples are presented chronologically.

Example 1 A non-controversial study: student routes through the B.Ed.

In so far as it was not complicated by controversy this study provides a useful preliminary illustration of the basic evaluation machinery working as intended.

The focus of this study was requested by the B.Ed. course committee who proposed that the evaluation committee should 'analyse data already available relating to the programmes students are constructing for themselves with a view to establishing what patterns are emerging, particularly in relation to students' professional intention'. No purpose-built instruments were required for this study — the data was available in the form of student records and it simply had to be analysed. The combinations of units were analysed by the research assistant and four main patterns were identified.

The ten-page report was disseminated as indicated above. It offered four sorts of analysis. Firstly, head-counting:

□ *Subjects taken by over 25 per cent of students in any age range at foundation level.*

Subject	Mental Handicap	Primary I	Primary II	Secondary
	%	%	%	%
Mathematics	60	83	82	39
Psychology	48	63	43	32
Religion	48	40	(24)	57
Philosophy	44	33	27	36
Literature	32	27	34	43
Sociology	28	(7)	(3)	(6)
Sciences	28	30	40	24
Art	(16)	33	(18)	(14)
etc.				

□

Secondly, an attempt to identify patterns of student subject choices:

□ Category 1 *The 'One-subject' student*

That is the student whose subject choices shows a clear single elective subject, which he carries through each stage of the course. To be classified in this group, the same subject must appear as B, C and D or E Unit. Also, if the subject is not taken as an F Unit, it must have been taken at 'A' level.

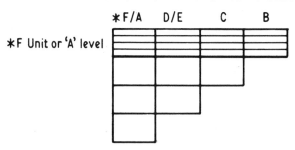

Category 2 *The 'Specialist'*

This category is really a more specialized sub-group of category 1. To be included, the student must have a single subject as defined above, and also have done additional D/E or C unit(s) in that subject.

Category 3 *The 'Two-subject' student*

These students have a first subject as described above and also a second subject, followed through in the same way and taken as a C unit. Also included are a few students who studied only two subjects beyond foundation level, although one or both of these may have first been taken as D or E units.

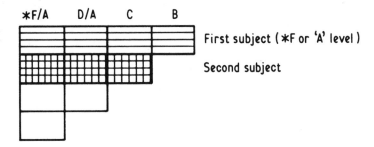

First subject (*F or 'A' level)

Second subject

Category 4 *The 'Generalist' or non-specialist*

These students do not follow a subject right through, as described above. They tend to take units in more subjects. ▫

Thirdly, a straightforward summary having the style of the following extract:

☐ 1 80% of the students sampled still intend to teach the same age group as when they started at college.
  2 47% of students provisionally intend to take a B unit in the subject they offered at interview.
  3 73% of students have taken a C unit in a subject taken at 'A' level, and 56% are intending to do a B unit in one of their 'A' level subjects.
  4 Only 16% are doing what we have termed 'generalist' programmes having equal emphasis on more than two subjects. However 27% of all students are in the 'one-subject' category, and the majority of these fill the remainder of their programme with a wide range of subjects.
  etc.   ☐

Finally, some tentative speculations to provoke discussion of the data. For example:

☐ It may seem that many students are choosing traditionally: that is to say, that although we have deliberately avoided the use of terms like 'main' and 'subsidiary' hitherto, student routes quite similar to the former main/subsidiary pattern are popular. At the same time there are some differences in the extent of such specialization as between primary and secondary students, and marked differences between age-ranges in the most popular subjects. In a sense this vindicates the view that the markedly different characters of primary and secondary schools require that students have the opportunity, not merely of subject choice in a fixed structure, but of structural flexibility and differentiation in the elective/academic area as well as in their professional studies.

Nevertheless, given the limited extent of such differentiation in actual student choices, we should ask ourselves whether our students are making maximum use of the flexibility the course offers, and in particular whether primary students have grasped the relationship between the opportunity to diversify and the particular characteristics of the primary school curriculum.
  etc.   ☐

This report was well-received in the college. The B.Ed. course committee was particularly pleased with it since having requested the study in anticipation of a visit by HMI they found that it produced data which was impressively detailed and findings which were highly supportive to the new course's rationale and organization. Moreover, it required no immediate action: as they pointed out, 'It was felt that its main contribution could be to the initial planning of a new B.Ed.' The ultimate accolade was HMI 'interest in E28 (the report on this study) because of its relevance to the problem of re-orientation of students' choice'.

This study was a significant success in that it showed the evaluation programme to be producing information which was constructive, non-threatening yet of a sufficient depth and novelty of insight to provide food for thought and not to be dismissed on the grounds that 'we know this already'.

The success of this study tended to be confirmed by subsequent evaluation exercises. A follow-up interview programme proved to be problematic, but the more neutral method of records analysis was used to follow the patterns of student choice into the optional honours year of the course. A further and final analysis of the complete cycle of academic choices from 'A' levels, through each year of the course to the final units, was then undertaken. Both these studies used the same sample of students as in the original study, and the three linked studies thus provided detailed and comprehensive data on the academic careers of a cohort of students over five years of exercising choice, the latter stages of which necessarily related to their varying conceptions of professional need.

Example 2 A comprehensive study invoking a wide range of participant perspectives: Professional Studies in the B.Ed.

As the new B.Ed. took an approach to Professional Studies which, for the college and the time, was quite radical, no special case needed to be made for giving Professional Studies priority in the 1975–6 B.Ed. evaluation programme. The focus was stated in the approved programme for that year as follows:

☐ 1 It is recommended that in view of the pivotal and innovatory nature of second-year professional studies (CP) it should provide the major focus for B.Ed. course evaluation during 1975–6. Such evaluation should concentrate upon two critical aspects of these units: school and college, and team operation.

1.1 *School and college* School experience is intended to have a degree of integration with college-based studies considerably greater than in previous courses, and to involve students, tutors and teachers in new relationships and new ways of working. Responses to the philosophical basis of school experience, to its operation, to the new roles required and to the relationship between school and college-based work will be sought directly from each group of participants — tutors, students and teachers in schools — via instruments to be developed during the year.

1.2 *Team operation of CP* CP units depend for their success to a great extent on staff with varying specialist skills working together in new ways. It is intended to explore how such a team approach to planning and teaching is working in practice and to undertake such exploration through the team organization itself. CP unit leaders will be asked to cover, as part of the frequent team discussions they will be undertaking in any case, certain topics relating to the organization of CP and contributing tutors' responses to it, with a view to producing statements for analysis incorporating the range of views expressed. It is hoped that this approach will not only provide useful insights once completed but will also make a positive contribution while the units are running; at the same time the demand of this approach on staff time is minimal. The possibility of making available a structured response instrument in addition to the above for tutors who wish to supplement the team discussions with individual perspectives is to be explored. □

This study turned out to be more comprehensive in investigative scope and more complex in administration than was anticipated. At the same time it stands in retrospect as perhaps the best example the programme produced of evaluation working in practice as had been intended. In particular, there was a high level of participation by staff and students and some of the significant course changes which followed the evaluation were demonstrably the direct outcome of the evaluation process and its findings.

One of the basic difficulties here was the scale of the course components to be investigated. They involved 322 students, thirty-three full and part-time staff working on four course units which, while sharing an overall 'professional' philosophy in the form of a set of governing principles and forty-three pre-specified instructional objectives, were organized in very different ways. Moreover, the units had a substantial school-based component in the form of regular days in school together with a block something akin to the traditional 'school practice'. The school-based work served a resource-cum-workshop role which was vital to the success of the integration ideology of the rationale, yet of course its actual conduct was only partly under college control, for — naturally — students working in schools do so at the head's invitation, on the school's terms and in a manner which causes minimal disruption to the school's primary obligation to its pupils. So the success of these units depended to a considerable extent on factors which were out of the college's hands — the level of understanding of school staff of the new ideas of school experience and the changed roles for students, tutors and school staff, the commitment accorded to such ideas and roles, the extent to which a school's organization and ethos served to facilitate the observational and executive tasks given to the students, and so on.

In the event methodology and organization of the study proceeded on what might in some respects seem like an *ad hoc* basis. There was no 'grand design' at first, and the focus shifted from one part of the study to the next, according to the way issues emerged which were seen as significant and worthy of further exploration. Theoretically, this style can be dignified by reference to the 'responsive' mode of Stake (1976) and the 'progressive focusing' approach of illuminative evaluation (Parlett and Hamilton, 1972) and the openness and flexibility of its design was entirely consistent with the college's evaluation constitution. However, it did pose a challenge to the tight control clauses in the constitution and the evaluation committee's terms of reference, for in effect the academic board approved a limited focus and the actual studies concentrated on additional issues not approved by the board in advance.

The first part of the study consisted of an extensive structured questionnaire, devised by a working group consisting of the evaluation officers, the co-ordinator of Professional Studies and the president of the students' union. This covered the two areas specified in the agreed programme but it was decided to take advantage of the opportunity to expand it into a comprehensive feedback schedule covering all major aspects of the course units. In particular the questionnaire invited students to react in various ways to the forty-three Professional Studies objectives — ranking them as perceived to be (a) important and (b) achieved, and this addition provided findings which were held to be highly significant and were followed up in subsequent stages. For example:

☐ *Effectiveness in providing for teaching and learning at a basic level*

	This is important at this stage	Not important at this stage	Developed to a basic level by this stage	Not yet de- veloped
Ability to devise appropriate objectives for the classroom				
Ability to apply insights derived from study of children's development				
Ability to apply insights derived from study of social and environmental influences on children				
Ability to apply learning and teaching theories when planning for the classroom				
Ability to apply insights gained from observing classrooms and children				
Awareness of a range of approaches to planning classroom activities				
Awareness of a range of available teaching and learning resources				
etc.				

The questionnaire was administered by unit staff and following analysis the data was presented to those staff in the form of percentage responses on a blank copy of the questionnaire as shown below. As the covering note to staff emphasized, the data was left in this form to encourage staff and students to deepen their involvement in the

☐ *Attitudes and relationships with children and adults*

	Important	Not important	Developed to a basic level	Not yet developed
Ability to communicate easily with children	100	–	83	10
Ability to respond to children	100	–	87	6
Ability to gain children's confidence	100	–	74	19
Ability to gain children's co-operation	100	–	75	17
Ability to organize purposeful learning activities for children	96	3	96	26
Ability to relate to and work with children from varying abilities and backgrounds	95	5	52	+43
Ability to work co-operatively with other adults	91	6	78	17
Ability to accept advice and criticism	96	3	88	6
Ability to respond to — and act upon — advice and criticism	96	3	87	8
etc				

————————————————————————————————☐

evaluation process by offering their own interpretations, explanations and recommendations, and staff did in fact respond to this invitation in considerable detail.

Such participant involvement in the process of interpreting and explaining data in this case serves to secure not only commitment to the evaluation process but, more fundamentally, an understanding of the complexity of the epistemological issues underlying all such attempts to seek 'information' about educational events. For example, a basic question raised by the data above is whether one accepts that if a student says he can communicate easily with children he really can. For apart from the vagueness of the word 'communication', it should be apparent that such data might say as much about a student's capacity for self-appraisal as it does about the effectiveness of his course. The extent to which this basic point is not grasped in evaluation studies using student feedback instruments is disturbing. No feedback statement is of itself a fact: the only fact in the exercise is that a student has put a tick in a box.

In this case, while student responses on many issues provoked comment among staff and subsequent discussion and action, it was the outcome of the questions on objectives which produced most interest. For what emerged was a clear gulf between the college's 'model' of the teacher as one who acts on the basis of rational appraisal of alternatives and a fund of pedagogical knowledge and principles, and the students' almost exclusive concern with the most overtly 'practical' elements in teaching. As one tutor commented:

☐ In terms of agreed specific objectives the students see the unit as . . . not unsuccessful. However, in terms of what students regard as the *proper* objectives of professional studies the unit has performed less than adequately. . . . The gulf seems as wide as ever between what we in teacher education consider the new entrant to the profession requires, and what the nineteen- or twenty-year-old aspirant to professional status is convinced we should provide him with. . . . How can we persuade a greater proportion of students that teaching is thinking as well as action? ☐

The issue was taken up in the second part of the study, as a schedule completed by tutors. This would have been better as a structured questionnaire: it took its final form — as a loose schedule with thirteen broad headings under which comment was invited — simply because this form was the most acceptable to staff. The headings themselves were suggested by tutors after discussion at tutorial team level:

☐ 1 *Responsibilities within the tutorial team*
e.g. the handling of detailed planning and administration; the allocation of individual planning and teaching responsibilities; parity, equity; availability of expertise.

2 *Team co-operation in preparation and feedback*
e.g. contribution of other members of the team to the preparation of your material; adequacy of feedback from the rest of the team; workload involved in preparing your material; realism of time-scale.

3 *Presentation to students of material planned by others*
e.g. problems encountered in helping students with material prepared or presented by other team members; clarity and ease of use of material offered by others; adequacy of time available to prepare and discuss it before giving it to the students; extent and ways in which you feel you have been able to make a contribution to the development of other team members' parts of the unit; extent to which you felt able to cope with specialist material.

4 *Tutors' roles in relation to tutorial groups: what these were and the problems they presented.*
e.g. in relation to: seminar work; organizing and supervising; marking assignments; school experience; general help and support.

5 *Tutors' roles in the team as a whole*
i.e. the collection of roles that emerged and the extent to which these were congruent with the intended 'team-based' approach.

6 *Student reactions to the unit's organization*
e.g. the extent to which your group seemed happy with the way the unit was organized — content, tutorials, team operation, etc.

7 *The integration of school and college studies*
e.g. adequacy of preparatory contact between school and college; extent of heads'/teachers' understanding of and commitment to the new pattern of school experience; extent of team integration of tutors, teachers and students; degree of co-ordination of college studies and students' tasks for day visits.

8 *Objectives of the unit and of its school experience component*
e.g. appropriateness, realism, etc.

9 *Relative importance of objectives*
   In the Professional Studies student questionnaire students were
   asked to indicate which of the objectives they felt to be most
   important. It would be useful to establish whether there are
   notable differences between tutors and students on this. Would
   you please list your own priorities — please give not more than
   ten. How far do you feel the unit has fulfilled these particular
   objectives?

10 *Unit content*
   e.g. appropriateness, content, etc.

11 *Comments on teaching methods*
   e.g. the appropriateness of various teaching methods as used
   this year; mass lectures; video-tapes; seminars, etc.

12 *Student response to the unit as demonstrated by their written
   work, activities in schools and contributions to discussion*
   e.g. levels of understanding displayed in assignments; quality
   of contributions to discussion; classroom executive skills; any
   comparisons you wish to make with previous generations of
   students at a comparable stage.

13 *Other comments*   □

The responses to this schedule were full and provocative. The objectives issue was confirmed and explored more deeply and provided
additional data for later stages of the study. Again the report on this
procedure offered no interpretation: merely the raw data reorganized
into more readily assimilable form, with a separate report for each of
the four units as the following extract exemplifies:

□ *Problems of presenting other people's material*

1 There is something very unsatisfactory about trying to teach
   other people's material. We don't discuss methods as a team —
   but wait to be told by the member responsible what to do.

2 Not always clear instructions. (3)

3 Generally clear. (3)

4 Varies. (1)

5 Could use more time to prepare it. (5)

6 Usually enough time. (1)

etc.   □

This interim report did, however, set alongside each other student
and tutor rating of course objectives to encourage discussion:

☐ *Relative importance of course objectives*

The most frequently mentioned were:	Staff	Students
1 Ability to organize purposeful learning activities for children	(5)	(53%)
2 Ability to assess children's development and capabilities	(4)	(40%)
3 Ability to apply insights gained from observing classrooms and children	(4)	(10%)
4 Ability to communicate easily with children	(4)	(64%)
5 Ability to gain children's co-operation etc.	(4)	(43%)

☐

The third part of the Professional Studies evaluation was an attempt to tap the views of the remaining group of participants in the course, heads and teachers in associated schools. Questionnaires devised by course unit leaders were supplemented by detailed reports made at a series of meetings between school and college teachers in the college during the second half of the academic year. As a method of evaluation, the most serious problem here is that the sensitivity of the relationship between schools and colleges (particularly the fact that colleges depend on schools' goodwill for students' school places) can inhibit the frank exchange of views. On the other hand, face-to-face sessions can be as educative to the parties involved as the reports are expected to be to their readers. The reporting style was similar to the one exemplified above.

By this stage we had a large collection of reports dealing with data collected from three sources — staff, students and school teachers — and dealing with both college-based and school-based work in each of the four professional units. The next task was to pull all of this together into a coherent commentary. The final report was 46 pages long, listed all methods, numbers and composition of respondents and reports from each contributory stage and identified the four dominant themes which, regardless of the original brief from the academic board, the study had actually concentrated on (these included the two 'approved' areas of (1) school/college relations and school experience (2) staff roles within the college tutorial teams, together with the emergent themes of course objectives and teaching methods).

For each of the four themes the different perspectives were juxtaposed, both on a quantitative basis in the form of tables of response figures/percentages, and in summary form. For example:

☐ Both tutors and students agree on the importance of objectives very basic to the teacher's role: co-operation and communication with children; planning a range of classroom activities; being aware of children's development.

Beyond this, however, tutors and students tend to emphasize rather different kinds of objectives. Students select other objectives concerned with the development of relationships with children, and the ability to learn from advice and criticism. Also, they emphasize self-criticism and confidence at work.

Tutors, on the other hand, emphasize objectives relating to analysis and interpretation of classroom activities, of problems relating to teaching and learning etc; they appear to be particularly concerned to promote in students the ability to intellectualize classroom concerns.

etc. ☐

From a methodological standpoint the juxtaposition of such diverse material on an intuitive, *ex post hoc* basis may be regarded in some quarters as questionable, but as the report's conclusion argued, 'Choosing methods is essentially a pragmatic affair — we have to use those which our colleagues are prepared to countenance and participate in.' Moreover, since the function of the studies was to identify and juxtapose participant perceptions as a basis for staff discussion and course improvement, rather than to 'prove' course success or failure, such an approach seemed defensible. The report went on:

☐ What we now have is a very wide range of expectations, perceptions and reactions, both within and between categories of participants. . . . It (the evaluation) provides a commentary upon (though not a test of) the hypothesis that some 'problems' in teacher education are a direct product of the conflicting expectations which students, tutors and teachers in schools hold about teacher education courses. . . . ☐

As must be clear by now, this succession of related evaluation studies introduced new complexities into the hitherto simple production-line formula for evaluation. For there were interim reports as well as a final report, and much of the 'application' took the form not of course modifications but of further evaluation studies to explore particular issues more deeply or from a different participant viewpoint. Interim reports were made available in the established way — to staff concerned, to the evaluation committee, the B.Ed. course committee and the students' union, and on each a summary was produced for the academic board. The final report was dealt with in the same way, but in addition separate and selective summaries were produced firstly for mass student consumption and secondly for the information of schools which had participated in the evaluations. Both these documents avoided tables and lengthy interpretation, aiming for clarity and brevity, as the following extract from the students' report shows:

☐ *Teaching methods*   Students felt that school experience, group seminars and discussion contributed to the achievement of unit objectives more than any other activities. (Lectures, reading and films were said to contribute least.) Tutors also seemed to agree that seminar work had been the most valuable teaching method. Seven tutors said they were aware that mass lectures had been unpopular with students — but some emphasized that these could be very valuable if well prepared and well presented to not too large groups of students. Some tutors also mentioned the value of individual tutorial work, but felt they had too many students to do as much of this as they would like.

School experience   Students felt they were more successful in achieving school experience objectives concerned with establishing working relationships with children, and teachers, and experiencing the various aspects of a teacher's role. They found it more difficult to analyse and apply theory to the school situation.

Some 75% of students had some difficulty in relating their college-based studies to their work in school — as we saw earlier, students would like more emphasis on curriculum work, classroom problems etc. at this stage. Also some teachers in schools felt that the college should place more emphasis on curriculum content, visual aids etc. — they felt that they had to give students too much help with the content and organization of their lessons.

etc.   □

The proponents of the college's evaluation programme were now faced with a major challenge: to demonstrate that this considerable exercise, which had produced lengthy documents and had involved the time of large numbers of staff, students and school teachers,[1] had produced course improvements of a type which could not have been engendered by the normal evolutionary process. The argument that the 'impact' of an evaluation is more properly judged in terms of the extent to which it promotes a climate of careful critical appraisal of courses, teaching and learning — the 'theorizing institution' — than in terms of tangibles like the more obvious course modifications, only cuts ice in settings where such a climate already exists. Elsewhere — and this college was no exception — 'impact' is measured on a cruder, short-term cost-effective basis. Fortunately for the programme's credibility, we were able to demonstrate clear and substantial modifications to the professional units and their associated school experience which were directly attributable to the evaluation studies and these were reported in the follow-up documentation.

Extract from follow-up report on Professional Studies evaluation:

□ Unit content and the sequence of topics have been re-ordered to bring about a clearer focus on, and greater prominence to, those objectives that last year's experience and the evaluation procedures have shown to be central. Greater definition has been given to the term 'curriculum' by examining general issues in closer relationship to major areas of the junior school curriculum — this should go some considerable way towards meeting expressed student need for greater guidance in classroom skills without loss to the essential concepts of second-year Professional Studies.

A number of organizational changes will be effected: attempts will be made to bring about more direct tutor contact with class teachers; mass lectures will be avoided wherever possible; school experience tasks will be made more open-ended and flexible, and more 'curriculum' focused.

etc.   □

Example 3   A study in a highly sensitive area: student workloads

The new B.Ed. course offered a wide range of choice from a large number of units. Considerable effort had gone into attempting to secure parity of assessment and workload, but by the end of the first year of the new course the view was being voiced by many students and certain staff that students were being given in some cases vastly excessive workloads in terms of the agreed norm, and in others they were getting by with insufficient work.

Extract from B.Ed. course committee memo:

☐ The student view has been expressed on a number of occasions to the committee. Some comments have been

1 that not enough private work has been given — or if it has been given, it has not been apparent how much time and effort or indeed what strategies were needed;

2 that the amount of 'free' time in a week is both overwhelming and bewildering after a school time-table;

3 that the uneven incidence of work (both between units and with time through a unit) has caused strain;

4 that some units are regarded as exacting, while others might be labelled 'soft options'.

etc.   ☐

Either way this affected all teachers on these units. Staff responsible for more demanding units resented the possible loss of students to 'soft options' while those somewhere near the norm felt that students were being forced to devote insufficient time to their particular units because of excessive demands from elsewhere.

Finally, the B.Ed. course committee, which found itself the target of these complaints, forwarded a request to the evaluation committee that the matter be investigated. Although foci for that year's evaluation programme were already agreed, the committee set up a working party of staff and students to consider possible ways of investigating the problem. This group identified the methodological complexity of the task (does one define workload as time taken or effort expended? what allowance is made for variation in student abilities and motivation?) and produced a draft questionnaire. The study was included in the evaluation programme for the following academic year approved by the academic board.

The final version of the questionnaire was then completed and arrangements were made for its administration.

Extracts from workload questionnaire:

☐ 1 It is anticipated that, in addition to time spent in lectures etc. each 'D' or 'E' unit should involve approximately six hours spent in private study each week. Bearing this in mind, and looking back over the unit as a whole, how demanding was each D and E unit that you took in terms of the amount of work (both assessed and non-assessed) required by the tutor for successful completion of the unit? . . . In the final column please give an estimate of the number of hours per week spent on each unit.

Unit number	The unit should have demanded more work	About right	Too demanding	It was a real strain to meet the demands of the unit	Approximate number of hours spent per week

2 Which of these units demanded least work? Unit number . . . .
Which of these units demanded most work? Unit number . . . .

3 Do you feel that your work in any of your D and E units frequently suffered because of the demands of other units? No . . . Yes . . . Unit(s) . . . . suffered because of the demands of Unit(s) . . . .

4 In any unit, the work is rarely distributed completely evenly throughout the unit's length. Thinking back over your D and E units, please indicate with a tick on the time-scale following, any particular points at which the pressure of work on a specific unit was particularly great. If possible also state briefly the reason for this pressure.

etc. ☐

This study was not only complex methodologically but highly sensitive politically. Both factors dictated a more cautious and lengthy progress than had been achieved in the student routes study. At its first meeting of 1976–7 the committee felt that it could not resolve alone the vital matter of whether individual units should be publicly identified in the study and the ensuing report (without such identification the study would be so general as to be useless as a basis for rectifying the problem). Accordingly a report was sent to the academic board which outlined the difficulties and invited the board to choose between three options:

Extract from evaluation committee interim report to the academic board.

☐ 1 The report can identify individual units, indicating the perceived levels and characteristics of workloads, in the body of the report.

2 The report can provide a description in general terms of the incidence of heavy/light/average workloads, of the sorts of activities found excessively demanding or undemanding, the incidence of pressure points and the like. Information on individual units can then be made available on a confidential basis to the unit leaders concerned, and to them only.

3 The report can provide a description in general terms and make no reference to individual units; nor would it be supplemented by any such information.

While the evaluation committee seeks board guidance on the options listed above, it wishes to point out that the study makes little sense methodologically unless the questionnaire invites students to identify individual units taken. . . . It could also be argued that a report on workloads at the level of generality of 3 above would be valueless since it could not serve as a basis for action to improve the situation.
etc. ☐

As might be expected, the board agreed to discrimination between units in the questionnaire, and identification of units in the report.

The report was lengthy (thirty-four pages) and detailed, indicating general tendencies and identifying units which appeared

to demand insufficient work,
to demand far too little work,

to demand too much work,

to demand excessive non-assessible work over and above the formal assessment requirements,

to have undue assessment pressure at particular points in the academic year.

Aggregated, such results had clear implications for the college's over-all assessment policy. Extract from workloads report:

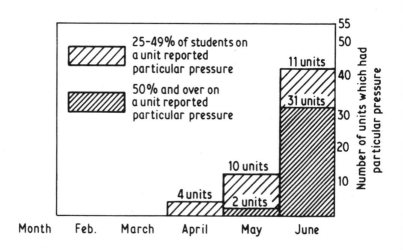

Clearly there is some congestion of work on D and E units during June which is to some extent inevitable. However, a number of units seem to achieve a fairly even spread of work. Over half the students reported no period of particular pressure on 21 of the 55 D and E units.

These results were linked to analyses of the perceived levels of difficulty of units and students' motivation for choosing the units they did. Copies of this report went to all unit leaders involved in the study and a summary was forwarded to the academic board. Copies of all this material was made publicly available in the usual way.

However, the committee did exercise discretion over one matter; detailed breakdowns of the responses for each unit, including verbatim responses to open questions, were sent only to the staff concerned, for it was argued in committee that this sort of detail could prove needlessly embarrassing to individual tutors: the function of the evaluation programme was to support the teaching staff's efforts, not to undermine them.

Extract from a workloads report on an individual unit:

☐ 1 This subject was taken at 'A' level by 23 students on the unit
  2 This subject was *not* taken at 'A' level by 5 students on the unit.
  3 This subject was taken as a Foundation unit by 17 students on the unit.
  4 This subject was *not* taken as a Foundation unit by 11 students on the unit.
  5 Not all the work done in D and E units is assessable. Even so, this non-assessable work may be compulsory. Please indicate any categories of non-assessable work which you felt *demanded too much of your time*:

Seminar preparation	2
Reading	7
Visits	2
Field work/practical work	
other	
etc.	☐

Again, we stress the significance of presenting as much data as possible in raw (but comprehensible) form so that the onus was on the tutor to offer interpretations and explanations, to theorize about his own teaching and his students' responses to it. Why, for instance, in a literature unit (which the above extract relates to) should a significant number of students see the basic activity of reading as making excessive demands on their time?

Not surprisingly, little feedback was received about changes made in the light of this study. The B.Ed. course committee welcomed the report, and thereafter it was accepted that tutors would make such modifications as were necessitated by the study at a private level. That such changes were made there was little doubt however, and in any event the issue was successfully defused, for the central general finding of the study was that while there was disparity of workloads between units, it was nothing like as extensive as had been portrayed. In this case an evaluation study could be seen to provide a more rational and evidential basis for discourse than the rumour and innuendo which had stimulated the study: a preferred alternative in the end, despite the initial unease about 'exposure' of individual staff.

Example 4   The problem of unpalatable findings: the students' routes follow-up study

The first study discussed here was an analysis of existing data on students' choice of units and their various 'routes' through the B.Ed. This study produced conclusions which were felt to be generally illuminating, helpful and supportive, and the idea of trying to probe beyond patterns of student routes, to seek explanations, causes and motives, received full support from the B.Ed. and evaluation committees. Accordingly, it was written into the 1976–7 draft programme and approved by the academic board:

☐ Follow-up study on student routes from 'A' levels to third-year B/BP units (see memo E28, circulated last year). The first study established *patterns* of routes; this will seek explanations for those patterns, possibly through an interview programme.   ☐

The commitment of the B.Ed. course committee to the study was further demonstrated in their preparedness to undertake the interviewing of students, which it was felt would be the most appropriate method. A draft interview schedule was prepared by the evaluation officers and this was then revised in the light of discussion in both committees. A sample of interviewees representative of the various 'routes' identified in the earlier study, and of the standard college variables of sex, professional intention and subject background, was invited to participate. Interviewees were allocated to tutors with whom they had had no tutorial or personal contact, dates were agreed and the interviews were conducted over a period of several weeks during the latter part of the autumn term. All interviews were tape recorded except in the one case where an interviewee requested otherwise.

Extracts from student routes follow-up interview schedule 'Instructions to interviewer':

☐ 1 Areas of discussion to be covered during the interview are

introduced by a broad open-ended question. These are underlined.

2 It is suggested that the interviewer allows the student to respond
spontaneously to this broad question.

3 Most of the introductory questions are followed by further subsidiary questions. When the student has finished answering the
opening question, it is suggested that the interviewer checks
whether his/her answer has covered all these points in sufficient
depth. If not, the interviewer should ask some supplementary
questions.

4 Some questions are followed by examples of the kinds of answers
that might be given, although we do not know the full range of
answers that is possible. These are to help the interviewer to
understand the purpose of the question, so that he can explain it
to the student, if necessary. Strictly speaking, such examples
should not be used as 'prompts' if students offer no reply,
because they are, of course, a kind of leading question. However,
they may help the interviewer to rephrase the question, or be
used in illustration if essential.

etc.   □

Examples of questions:

□ *The pattern of subjects taken*

We shall explain to the student how we have categorized the
patterns of the unit choices, and which category he/she falls
into.

Q.1   *When choosing your foundation and elective units, were you
conscious of trying to build a pattern of related units, or of trying to
achieve such a balance/mix of subjects?*

Did you plan to follow one or two subjects right through your unit
options? Did you plan to specialize/cover a broad range of subjects
as far as possible?

Was it a planned/or an *ad hoc* combination of units?

Q.2   (If the answer to Q.1 was *yes*) *at what stage did you plan
this?*

Did you intend it right from the start, or did the pattern change/
develop at a later stage? Or did it emerge by building on previous
units, step by step?

Q.3 *What were your reasons for combining the units in this way/for taking this balance of different subjects?*

In what way did you intend it to meet your personal needs? (academic or otherwise)?

In what way did you consider this pattern appropriate for your professional requirements (for the age-range you intend to teach)?

Which was more important to you — to use the units for personal or professional needs?

Were you aware of any intention the college might have for your use of Foundation and Elective units? Did this influence your choice? (e.g. was it intended for 'liberal education', 'academic development', 'professional background' etc.)

Was your choice of units and the balance/mixture of subjects you took affected by guidance from tutors? Do you feel you had enough guidance on this? If not, what kind of advice do you feel that you lacked?

etc. ☐

In all, the schedule had twenty-two questions. Interviewers were encouraged to diverge from these where appropriate, but overall, although interviewer style and competence varied (particularly in the extent to which the subsidiary questions were used in a leading way), the interviews mostly covered the same ground.

Although, as can be expected from a study involving nine interviewers all of whom had full commitments elsewhere, there were some administrative difficulties, by and large this study was remarkably successful up to this point, and both the evaluation and B.Ed. course committees commented on the significance of the partnership which had been engendered.

Analysis of all the tapes was of course a lengthy and demanding activity, but it was completed on time, and four reports were produced, covering the main issues which emerged from the analysis.

The reports and summaries were made widely available in the normal way. They were very full (eight, thirty, eighteen and nine pages respectively) but the reporting style reflected what we had learned from earlier studies about ways of combining detail with readability (e.g. like the use of colour-coding for summaries and background information). The reports are divided into sections, each dealing with a broad theme. The reader is offered a brief summary of the main points emerging under the theme, supported by a lengthy sample of the verbatim quotations on which this summary statement is based. The quotations allow the reader to judge the accuracy of the summary, yet also to see the individuality of each response and offer his own interpretations. Where appropriate the answers are categorized according to the four dominant student routes which emerged from the earlier study (see example 1 in this chapter, pp. 63–7). Extract from one of the four routes follow-up reports:

☐ *Students' views of the appropriateness of their pattern of foundation and elective units for a teacher of their chosen age-range*

Most of the students interviewed felt that foundation and elective units were intended by the college to meet their personal, academic needs, rather than their professional needs. However, in many cases professional 'needs' did influence unit choice. Later in the interviews, students were asked:

Do you feel the combination of units which you took met your professional requirements?

Did it give a good background for a teacher of your chosen age-range?

Below are some answers from students in each of the age-ranges:

PRIMARY II

1 One-subject students

I don't know. . . . I think the psychology helps you to understand what's going on — in Professional Studies last year we only did a little psychology. I think that's quite useful.

Q. Do you think that matters? Do you think these units are intended to meet your personal or professional needs?

A. Both, I think. I think its got to be interesting to you — but I don't suppose it has to have any use in the junior school, but it's a good thing if it does.

***

Yes, I think it does — I have kept the P.E. as the main subject, but I have done maths and environmental science, not just followed one other subject through, so that diversified the subjects that I am capable of teaching, which is what you need at primary school.

***

I think perhaps I'm lacking in some of the drama and movement things, but I'm hoping to be doing that later on this year. I think that's about all I feel I'm lacking at the moment . . . you can extract bits from each unit to meet the needs of the junior school. I feel as though I've had a pretty good grounding in most things.

***

2 Specialist students

Children's literature definitely. Understanding drama, yes to some extent. The history (specialist subject) I'd say not . . . because I don't feel that my age group really understand history . . . especially in the depth that I've done it, and I can only give them an approximation of the depth to which I've studied it, which is an awful draw-back. . . . But then, you see, puppetry — the level at which we did it, they could never do — so I'd have to bring that down again.

etc.   □

And so on: for this particular question the number of sample answers is considerable.

So far this study had proceeded smoothly, and with an impressive level of cooperation between the groups concerned — the B.Ed. course committee (whose members did the interviewing), the Students' Union (who sanctioned and supported the demands on members' time) and the evaluation committee. The 'problematic' element appeared at the data analysis stage. For what the reports focused and commented upon was somewhat different from what some colleagues may have anticipated, and in particular three interview questions — one about course flexibility, another about the overall 'liberal education' rationale of the B.Ed. and a third about tutorial guidance, which had looked innocuous enough when buried among a large number of other very diverse questions on the interview schedule — produced responses from students of a scale and character that required two of the reports to be devoted to these issues alone. At this point, from being another 'monitoring' or 'fact-finding' study like the original students routes analysis, the follow-up study, by virtue of the way students chose to answer the questions, assumed the role of a challenge to some of the fundamental principles on which the degree had been constructed and identified inconsistencies in the relationship between the course as intended and approved and the course in action.

The following serves both as an illustration of the reporting style in general and, in its content, exemplifies the responses which one of the three problematic questions produced.

☐ *How far were students' choices of units influenced by guidance from tutors?*

'Within these general constraints (unit prescriptions and proscriptions) there is freedom for you to choose according to your inclination, interests and intentions, and you alone will be responsible for your choices. Guidance, as required, will be given by your tutors, but it will be for you to construct the sort of programme that best meets your needs as you see them.' (*First Year Student Handbook*)
'Guidance' was interpreted by both tutors and students in a variety of ways. Most students felt that explicit direction from tutors was minimal — they were left to make their own decisions. A number said that tutors would give them information if they asked for it, but most students felt that tutors never tried to influence their choice.

> I felt that the college was leaving me completely free to choose whatever I wished, and I really enjoyed the course because of that. I wasn't under any pressure at all.

***

> As I said, these routes were the greatest help to me — I can't remember receiving very much help from anybody — I know I was very bewildered and confused when I first arrived in college and I do remember quite distinctly sitting down in front of that board and planning — and it was from that I made my choice.

***

However, some students found that tutors inevitably gave not wholly neutral 'guidance', although, of course, they were free to ignore this.

> Obviously, whatever he says, he can't help it, his choice of words and descriptions must bias the way he talks about things. I think he'd have liked me to take the unit — because he's a member of the department.

***

> I was very much aware, during an F unit, that the tutor was trying to sell his D unit — he kept giving a plug at it, and in that respect I found that all through college.

***

I was under the impression that they offered this wide range so that we could choose more or less what we wanted to . . . until they said I'd have to take a history course if I wanted to teach history. (Secondary Generalist)

**

My tutor advised us that if we were wishing to teach in secondary, it would be better to specialize in a subject — if we were going to teach in primary perhaps it wasn't so important. (Primary I student)

**

Some students felt they would have liked more direction, to ensure that they did not put themselves at a disadvantage by taking units they could not do well in, or to ensure they took a combination of units which would be most useful for their teaching career.

There were some subjects where you felt you should have done the F unit really, I don't think you could just go into them. I don't think you could go into something like art at the C unit level and not have done the others.

**

I think really perhaps they should put more restriction on in a way, because I think it must be difficult for people to go into these units and have to do these exams at the end, or assessments, and pass them, especially say with something like geography.

**

Q. Do you feel that anybody should have guided you more positively?

A. Yes — to me it would seem to be a good idea — just speaking about myself, not other people — it would seem to be a good idea that students should have a fairly extensive battery of tests to see what areas might be useful to them — I know some people might object to this — but, I mean I think of areas which I am still very weak in — sort of general knowledge which influences the way I am able to deal with science subjects — which maybe I should have had some extra guidance in. I think it is possibly left too much to the individual student. (Mental Handicap student)

**

I would have liked more guidance I think. . . . My school tutor, I asked her what she thought would be better job-wise, which course to do. She was as helpful as she could be, but she more or less said it was up to you. . . . They don't want to be sort of accused of having responsibility do they? Of sort of guiding you, I don't suppose. I can understand that in a way. But I think with the job situation, I wish that I had kept biology on now, looking back at it. Then I could have taught it at secondary, because its a shortage subject. Well, they didn't know then, I don't suppose, what it was going to be like job-wise. But in a way I half wish I had got the choice there. (Primary I, Generalist student)

The range of tutorial interpretation of 'guidance' — from overt unit-plugging to bland neutrality — and students' own differing views on their needs for guidance, suggest that re-appraisal of this aspect of the course would be useful.
etc.   □

Following established procedure, the body most closely involved in the study was invited to comment on the issues raised in the reports and to suggest appropriate action at the same time as the reports were made generally available. In this case since the study was about the degree as a whole rather than a part of it like Professional Studies, the relevant body was the B.Ed. course committee.

At first this committee declined to comment. Eventually, after being reminded of its statutory obligations it forwarded a paper to the evaluation committee. Essentially the B.Ed. committee was dismissive of the study, despite its own considerable investment at an earlier stage. Several of the conclusions of the report were neutralized by the use of words like 'fascinating' and 'interesting' together with statements that such findings only confirmed what was known already. On one of the particular problems for students which emerged in the study (the wide variation in the quality of tutorial guidance on unit choice illustrated above) the B.Ed. committee stated:

□ It is perhaps worthwhile the course committee commenting upon the method chosen for this type of evaluation. It is presumably of value to allow students to talk in a semi-formal situation where the interview is structured to some extent by the interviewer. . . . It does . . . seem rather diffuse in that it tends to produce an 'on the one hand, but on the other hand' type of response, and a rigorous analysis of the decision-making process is unlikely to result from this type of evaluation method. One would require much closer data presented in a much fuller form for such research (*sic*) to be of particular value, other than merely to be of interest. ☐

On the study's conclusion that the evidence of these interviews suggested that there could well be many students who lacked the understanding of the degree's 'liberal education' rationale which had been deemed vital to their making intelligent choices of units and that for some students the actual character of the education may not have been in accordance with the strong 'process' orientation approved by the CNAA, the B.Ed. committee's response was to re-interpret the data 'to indicate the undoubted fact that students on the course are at least aware of the philosophy of the course'.

Following lengthy discussion of the evaluation reports and the B.Ed. committee's response to them, the evaluation committee issued its own statement which in turn was highly critical of the B.Ed. committee's response. On the matter of tutorial guidance, the evaluation committee chairman said:

☐ A careful reading of E58 (i.e. the report) suggests that the issue is rather more complex than directive versus non-directive guidance. . . . The concluding paragraph . . . suggests that reappraisal of this aspect of the course would be useful. The response of the B.Ed. course committee, however, is presented in terms which suggest that this point has been overlooked, or ignored, or set aside, and it appears to us that the opportunity to debate the efficiency of this aspect of couse management (written up in some length and in . . . detail in the original submission . . .), to demonstrate the course committee's awareness of expressed dissatisfaction, and to communicate to course participants its concern and attitude relative to it, have unfortunately been missed. ☐

And on the extent to which the 'liberal education' commitment in the validated course rationale was reflected in practice, the evaluation committee suggested that the course committee's assertion that students were 'aware of the philosophy of the course' was 'a rather optimistic reading of E59' (the evaluation report) and urged it to interpret the reaction/action requirement by not only inviting discussion at departmental level but also by documenting the outcome of such discussion and associated decisions.

Perhaps the most notable element in this sequence of events was that the B.Ed. committee had sponsored and supported this study,

and, most significantly, had done most of the interviewing themselves. Thus, the data they were now rejecting had been produced by
their own efforts and the perceptions and opinions they were dismis-
sing were responses to their own questions. The irony of the B.Ed.
committee's objections to the methodology of the study (apart from
that they had sanctioned and undertaken it) is that conventionally
such a study might be expected to produce bland responses generally
supportive of the committee as a result of their being in a position, as
interviewers, to load the questions to secure desired responses.

This study demonstrates just how vital were the 'control' clauses in
the constitution. The B.Ed. committee was given a substantial measure of control over parts of this study as we have shown, but at three
vital points control was out of their hands. Firstly, the methodology
decision: the interviews were tape recorded, so that the selective
recording of responses which can happen when the interviewer takes
notes was not a risk; and secondly, the transcripts from these tapes
were analysed by the evaluation officers, not by the B.Ed. committee
members, and they were also available to the college community as a
whole. Thirdly, the dissemination decision: the agreed evaluation
constitution, not the committee, determined the extent of dissemination (unrestricted). Had each decision been taken by the B.Ed.
committee it can be surmised that issues like the apparent inadequacy
of the course tutorial guidance system would never have been raised
or the report might have been suppressed by the committee. For that
system was devised by the member of staff who by this time had taken
over the chief executive role on the B.Ed. committee, and he continued to be responsible for the system's effective functioning. He also
wrote the 'committee' response to the study which was received by the
evaluation committee.

To us this study shows not only the importance of resolving control
questions in general in institutional evaluation programmes, but also
the wisdom of widely shared control coupled with open dissemination. For what is at stake is less the question of the dependence or
independence of the *evaluator* (which is the issue normally focused
on) but the integrity (or 'independence') of the evaluation *process*.
That integrity is put at risk in any evaluation strategy where control of
all the decisions is vested in a single group rather than in the course
community as a whole.

The evaluation committee also commented on the B.Ed. committee's criticisms of the apparent lack of rigour and conclusiveness of

interviewing as a method, by reference to the usual arguments about depth and sensitivity, and by stressing that quantitative proof of 'facts' about course success/failure was neither intended nor claimed:

☐ It was hoped that such a study would contribute further to staff sensitivity and awareness of the opportunities, constraints and problems of the B.Ed. course for individual students. To characterize this . . . as producing nothing more than an 'on the one hand, but on the other hand' position seems to us to fail completely to appreciate the point, and the eagerness of the course committee to dismiss the issues appears to us again to have frustrated the opportunity for constructive debate. . . . (The evaluation committee's) primary concern is that the outcome of evaluation procedures should be not only 'fascinating' and 'interesting' but also useful. Therefore we would welcome any constructive suggestions on methodology from the B.Ed. course committee.   ☐

Such suggestions were not forthcoming and the study was subsequently not referred to again by the B.Ed. committee, though it was available and read elsewhere in the college.

We discussed in chapter 1 the difficulty over defining the 'successful' evaluation. This study provided probably the richest source of insights yet available by that stage of the evaluation programme into how students were responding to the new course: inasmuch as it failed to provoke 'constructive debate' between and within the management bodies concerned it cannot, in the short term at least, be counted 'successful'. Yet it is worth juxtaposing the two student routes studies — the one above and its predecessor which identified the routes. If one considers together the quality of the data, the depth of insight offered, the sense of challenge to staff 'theorizing' capacities, the actual responses from course management offered in each case, it becomes less and less easy to compare the two studies in terms of success/failure.

It is worth noting that this study was not, despite the difficulties outlined above, the end of the college's exploration of student careers through the new B.Ed. course. Three further studies were undertaken on this topic: two used the records analysis techniques which had proved so successful in the original routes study, tracing patterns of academic choice, and relating them to professional intention and other variables, from 'A' levels to the final honours choice points. The third study used questionnaires to explore the motives, expectations and justifications of students opting to stay on for the fourth (honours) year. These later studies were undertaken as part of the fourth annual evaluation programme.

Example 5: The use of external consultants

The approved 1976–7 programme (following the usual discussion in departments, students' union, course committee and evaluation committee) included this focus:

☐ Liberal education and professional preparation — rationale and practice. An attempt will be made to ascertain what the degree as a whole means to its students. Methods: under discussion.   ☐

This did indeed present a methodological problem — how could one encompass so broad an objective in a limited evaluation study? A lengthy discussion paper was prepared setting out a range of possible approaches, and presenting the case for building up a picture of the current state of the course through a combination of student interviews by external consultants, a 'portrayal' evaluation based on close observation of a particular part of the course, and juxtaposing these with all other relevant 'whole course' data, especially the student routes follow-up interviews discussed in the previous section. The two central procedures — the use of external consultants on an exchange basis and our venturing into literary-critical modes of appraisal for the portrayal evaluation — were highly innovative for the college, and, we suspect, for any institutional evaluation.

Both procedures took a long time to set up, but eventually a series of interviews, with students both as individuals and in groups, was conducted by three colleagues from other institutions, all of whom had been involved in a major teacher education evaluation project. (The other side of this exchange — in which the Charlesford adviser on evaluation undertook an evaluation of part of an experimental B.Ed. course in another college, is reported in Whalley, 1980). At the same time our 'portrayal' evaluator, a former member of staff who had published in the literary criticism field, undertook an extended programme of observation of teaching sessions, informal discussion with staff and students and documentary analysis.

The methodology of both studies was approved by the B.Ed. committee, the academic board and the staff concerned as well as the evaluation committee.

A central condition of the exchange interviews was that the three interviewers were given total independence as to the conduct of the interviews and the format and content of reports. This they requested, but the evaluation committee, too, felt that it was important that no college body should be seen to interfere with or influence the processes or their outcomes. As a result the reports took a form which many regarded as inappropriate for the communication of interview data: they were in part commentaries, but did not quote any of the raw data in support of statements made, as the following extract shows:

☐ All the students I saw accepted, and in some cases welcomed, the fundamental distinction made between professional and non-professional courses. All accepted that non-professional courses were for their personal development; all had, to some degree at least, enjoyed the courses in year 1. About half of the students spontaneously mentioned these early courses being designed to introduce the students to an area of knowledge rather than to specific content (and had done so).

There was a consensus of opinion that, as the three years of the course went on, content for its own sake rather than as a paradigm became more important.

Many of the students said that they had taken a much wider range of courses than they would have imagined when they started. A number said that they had come to college expecting to do one subject and had in fact done something quite different. They were most appreciative of the wide range of options open to them at each choice point; but a number felt that the whole rationale of the course was threatened by the cut-back in courses being offered to students now on course.

One of the course objectives which interested me was to do with the student being aware of the nature of the course, and coming to an explicit understanding of the view of knowledge embodied in the course design. From my discussions I could not say that this had been achieved in all cases. There appears from the course description to be no point after Foundation Studies where this view of knowledge is deliberately considered, unless it be in the professional courses. The two areas are so separate in the students' perceptions, however, that if this is included in the professional courses, it seems to have had little impact. It seems to me inherently unlikely that most students will, with no guidance, come to an interview aware of the nature of knowledge. If the objective is considered important, perhaps there might be some direct consideration of it after year 1.

etc.   ☐

Clearly, reports which summarize and comment without offering evidence risk being suspected of bias: at the same time, as our consultants argued, the ethics of wanting to check (and perhaps reinterpret) evaluation data when one does not like the conclusions drawn from it are somewhat dubious, particularly when the consultants' professional claim to expertise in this area was a strong one. Moreover, as far as the students were concerned, the frankness of some interviews was conditional upon their anonymity being preserved and the tapes and transcripts not being made available in the college.

Yet the summary reports gave no opportunity for alternative interpretations, and none for readers to penetrate beneath the interviewers' analytical framework to the thoughts and perceptions of the students themselves. The limited potential of the summary report can be demonstrated if we juxtapose an extract from one of the consultants' interview transcripts on which the report drew. The extract provides some of the raw material for the final paragraph in the report extract above.

Extract from one of the group interviews/'seeded discussions' undertaken by external consultants:

☐ Q. That's a very different definition to the other one. To you, a liberal education, then, is how subjects inter-link?

A. Yes, the underlying methodology, or knowledge, whatever.

Q. Because that's a very different definition to the other we've just been given. (Turning to the student who had talked about adaptability and flexibility.) Your definition had nothing to do with subjects, had it?

A. No. I quite like this one — the definition given in the college prospectus: 'through a liberal education a student is expected to develop into a knowledgeable person, one who understands the thinking process he is using and the ways various subjects he studies relate.' It's like I said before about teaching in a vacuum.

A. Yes, it's the way, the sort of thinking process inherent in each subject. The way they're all inter-related. I feel that its very important for kids in school, or anyone, if they're going to be educated, to have this understanding. It's like History relates to everything else.

Q. So, a liberal education is a relating of subjects, a breaking down of barriers between subjects?

A. And an understanding of the various ways of thinking.

Q. That implies that there are different ways of thinking. What different ways of thinking are there? I think it's right to ask that because after all, I'm talking to people who are at the end of a course which has given them a liberal education. What are different ways of thinking?

A. Well, certainly there are different subject disciplines.

Q. But you said different ways of thinking.

A. Take one subject — one theme — approach it from very different points of view and the idea is that we understand one theme from different perspectives, which is a very important one and which I don't think most schools are particularly interested in, and probably most colleges of education haven't been in the past. Hopefully a liberal education helps you to be able to do that. The ways that different subjects approach a particular theme or area of knowledge, so they are inter-related, so you are educated broadly, instead of being just educated in the one — Geography or History, or something.

Q. Yes, I can see this getting of understanding of different subjects where they have bearing on one's own subject, the ways in which they inter-relate. In other words you are no longer a specialist in one subject, you see things in a much wider perspective — I can see that, but different ways of thinking — surely, you either think or don't think.

A. No, I don't agree with that. You see, if we take the scientist and the artist, one expects the scientist to think in a particular way — perhaps a more factual way. People, even in school, are expected, if they do science, to think in a factual way in order to achieve certain things at the end of it. While an artist, for example, would be expected to think in a more creative way. Now this is a fallacy, I think, that people do think in these ways. Yet they are expected to think in those ways.

etc.   □

The evaluation committee quickly perceived the relative weakness of the summary report — the more noted since the reports appeared soon after the routes follow-up reports (discussed on pp. 84–95) which summarized and interpreted data, but also provided representative quotations from the interview transcripts. The committee requested that the consultants now release the transcripts to enable the college to benefit fully from the study, but this the consultants felt unable to do since it would put at risk their confidentiality agreement with the students. The college had no alternative but to accept this judgement, and the consultants' reports were then circulated in the usual way. In this example, the importance of having control of the methodology and dissemination decisions vested in the evaluation committee was again demonstrated, though in a rather different way from the previous example: here the problem arose because the committee had signed away a part of that control as a condition of the consultancy 'contract'.

Clearly the potential of this study was not realized. The evaluation committee argued that:

☐ The raw material of the reports, the tape-recorded interviews, represents a massive source of student commentary on the course that is potentially of far greater value than the brief written reports presented and very much above the level of 'normal conversation' that the B.Ed. course committee presumes it to be.   ☐

Yet that raw material remained unavailable to college staff and students, and this probably confirmed the opinion of those staff who felt that the use of external interviewers offered no real advantages: in an 'evaluation of evaluation' study undertaken at the end of the SSRC-funded stage of the programme, staff generally supported the range and application of evaluation methods used, with the prominent exception of the use of outsiders; grounds for anxiety were such outsiders' unfamiliarity with the courses under scrutiny, rather than the issue of data availability discussed here.

If one invokes the criterion of methodological integrity which we discuss in chapter 6, the latter issue is considerably more serious; in any case it was precisely because external consultants were unfamiliar with the course that their perspective was seen as a valuable addition to an appraisal process which had hitherto drawn substantially on 'insider' viewpoints. Nor was this the only use of external perspectives: frequent use was made throughout the programme of the reactions and perceptions of teachers in schools within which students were working or for which they were being trained. Notwithstanding the fact that teachers in schools both could be critical of the new course and could sometimes ground such criticism in an inadequate grasp of the course's rationale and purposes, the serving-teacher perspective appeared to be accorded a greater legitimacy than that of the fellow-teacher educator: a matter of practical politics, perhaps.

It will be inferred from the foregoing that criticism of the exchange interviewers' report was to be anticipated and to some extent would be justified. However, the strength of the B.Ed. committee's dismissal of the reported findings may not have been anticipated. The consultants, the committee asserted:

□ raise issues with which the course committee has been familiar for some time. The range of comments seems scarcely to have been worth the trouble of bringing members of staff some distance in order to discuss what are little more than generalities. □

The response then reduces a number of fairly complex points in the report to what it terms are 'statements which are scarcely worth making', and strongly criticizes the use of outsiders 'who have had no share whatsoever in the planning . . . of the course'. The report was finally characterized as 'interesting . . . but of very limited value'.

Once again the evaluation committee responded by defending the methods while in this case admitting the deficiencies of summary reports (which was not in fact a point of issue for the B.Ed. committee):

□ We believe that the treatment of the reports by the course committee, defective though they may be, can hardly represent an adequate response to their contents . . . and we regret the generally dismissive tone used. □

Example 6 A portrayal evaluation: valid critique or poor journalism?

The other consultancy study at this time was totally different in character and outcome. It was problematic, but not in the sense used so far; that is, it did not generate controversy of a sort which proved counter-productive in terms of evaluation's capacity to promote educational development. On the contrary, it proceeded smoothly and aroused little controversy at whole-college and course-management levels because it was a sharply focused case study which was seen as offering no real challenge to the course's managers and planners. Its most obvious challenge was to the lecturer and students involved in the study and to the academic assumptions and practices of the college's approach to the teaching of English literature, and since these people readily accepted and responded to the challenge, there was no real 'problem' in the institutional sense. The study is included here to exemplify a different, methodological, 'problem'. All institutional evaluation is conducted under constraints of a sort which the mainstream educational researcher rarely has to contend with; methodological choices in institutional evaluation are compromises and the studies in this and the next chapter exemplify some typical constraints and compromises. But the portrayal evaluation was subject to none of these. The method was chosen for purely 'methodological' reasons, and the subjects of the case study participated co-operatively and with enthusiasm. The study can be used, then, to illustrate a different dimension of difficulty, the validity of the evaluator's claim to 'tell it as it is'. The study illustrates the epistemological 'problem' in a purer form than do other studies complicated by institutional difficulties. Moreover, by being an explicitly impressionistic 'subjective' study in the qualitative mode (see Willis, 1978; Eisner, 1979), it highlights in a more obvious way than does an interview or questionnaire study the subjectivity/objectivity, case-particular/generalization issues which are central to all evaluation and are frequently invoked as a basis for rejecting evaluation findings.

The background to this study was set out in the preamble to the evaluation report:

☐ For this study we commissioned a 'portrayal' evaluation. The rationale for this approach is discussed in the evaluation adviser's memorandum to the committee, to which when it was circulated was appended an article by Elliott Eisner ('The perceptive eye: towards the reformation of educational evaluation'). The key feature of such a portrayal evaluation was to be that it would make no attempt to conform to the methodology and constructs of the social sciences, which (even in the haphazard and eclectic procedures of the (Charlesford) evaluation) have a virtual monopoly of curriculum evaluation and educational research. . . . [Author's note: this was written in 1977.] Instead, the possibilities of deliberately non-social science perspectives (e.g. those of the literary critic) were to be explored, and it was anticipated that such an evaluation might not only further our understanding of the course (the concern of the evaluation committee) but also of evaluation processes (one of the SSRC project's concerns).

A former member of the English department, J. C., agreed, after several discussion sessions, to undertake the study for us. For various reasons, some administrative, some personal, but most to do with the nature of the exercise, we decided to concentrate on a particular unit in J.'s own subject area and to consider it in its own terms, in relation to the degree as whole, and in the context of current developments in the teaching of English in schools and higher education. We felt that while the fairly close scrutiny of one unit would not constitute a piece of 'whole course' evaluation, it would tell us quite a lot about the course as a whole because of the way every unit is to some extent constrained, or at least influenced, by the structure (and, supposedly, by the rationale) of the degree course as a whole.

It is most important that readers of this study are fully aware of the background that I have just outlined, and that they are willing to avoid judging it in terms of criteria that it makes no attempt to conform to — namely those of traditional empirical research in the social sciences. It should also be considered as but one part of our attempt to provide insights into the way the new B.Ed. is working out in practice — alongside all the other studies undertaken during the past three years and listed in memo E60.

In one respect, colleagues closely concerned with the Initial B.Ed. ought to find that the methodology of this study raises familiar issues: if the B.Ed. is concerned to involve students in an exploration of the nature of knowledge, an evaluation of part of the B.Ed. whose methodology itself raises issues concerned with the competing claims of, boundaries between, constructs and methods of different areas of knowledge, should surely be grist to the college's epistemological mill.
etc. ☐

The consultant worked intensively with the staff and students concerned over a whole term, observing teaching, interviewing (formally), chatting informally, immersing himself in both the B.Ed. course documentation and the reading material for the unit being studied. His final report is long, idiosyncratic, full of challenge and interest and far more readable than the usual dry format of evaluation reports. The extracts which follow show both reporting style and the sort of data which the evaluator gathered.

Some of the report is devoted to the consultant's statements of his views on educational research in general and evaluation in particular:

☐ So many examples of 'research', as teachers can testify, have a crudeness and speciousness that makes them no more convincing as a picture of concrete reality than astrology. One basic fallacy is to believe that methods applicable in the field of the natural sciences are suited to other areas of study, such as the social sciences. . . . I would say that, without some sort of prior commitment to, and involvement in, the aims of a course, it is almost impossible to represent a course as a living process of change. A set of statistics about classroom practice can tell us little about education for real; any more than a public opinion poll can define for us the workings of a political system.

My approach in the following pages implies that the humanities have more to offer in education than the natural sciences, as a model for the researcher and evaluator. I would argue this because, by their very nature, the artist, historian, etc. work from a 'committed' standpoint — and I don't intend 'commitment' to have here the narrowly political connotation it has tended to have since the 1930s. At this point I ought to say that the question of subjectivity versus objectivity has sometimes been grossly distorted by the 'scientific' researcher intent on keeping the claims of the arts and the humanities in the area of research at bay. The arts are *not* subjective in the way conveyed by some behaviourists, who represent them as being the area of the fanciful, the idiosyncratic, and the crudely emotional. I am not arguing that we should simply — lock, stock and barrel — take our picture of educational reality from, say, the great poets, novelists, and dramatists: only that they do have much to offer the researcher. Observation from the outside does not satisfy them: they attempt to 'see into the heart of things'. They work to a sense of the immeasurable complexity of individual and social life, but they begin and end with the knowledge that a final picture must elude them. They see social reality in terms of change and fluidity, and reject any simple typology of human character and behaviour.

But they work from, and to, a kind of wholeness of response — as Yeats put it, 'blood, flesh, and intellect running together', and they incorporate the minute representation of life-in-its-variousness into a human totality. And above all, they are 'committed'.
etc.   ☐

The consultant then offers his alternative:

☐ To achieve this commitment would mean a 'researcher' abandoning his tools of measurement and 'scientific' analysis, and instead, involving himself directly at a personal and imaginative level in the work of a group of students and their teacher over a lengthy period of time. The resulting piece of 'research' would be likely, I think, to take the form of continuous narrative, using speech, characterization, description, commentary, etc. One specific shape this could take might be that of the notebook, diary or journal. In these forms, we conduct a dialogue with ourselves, we test out hypotheses, we project our feelings, thoughts, impressions, and intuitions into a space somewhere between the private and the public. Above all, we take the kind of risks which are frowned on in the usual modes of public discourse, such as the essay or the report.

It is the notebook form I have adopted, in however crude a manner, in the following pages. During the period I was observing the Auden-Larkin course in progress, I jotted down my brief thoughts on the course, on the subject of school, college and university English teaching, and on the present position of the colleges of education. I made tapes of the tutor and his students talking in various situations, and I invited and received their written comments. I also compiled a mini-anthology of quotations from the writings of educationalists, literary critics, etc. which were relevant to what I was doing, and have placed them alongside my own half-formed contributions. The result is perhaps something of a patchwork quilt, but it was a form that suited me because it offered me the chance to be more 'personal' and tentative than other forms might have done, and whatever the limitations of my own short and sketchy effort, it still seems to me a form worth recommending to researchers into classroom practice. I suppose I could have re-shaped everything I wrote to make a discursive essay, but this would have implied a finality of attitude I don't feel, and I don't want to convey. I don't claim that the points I make are either original or represent deeply considered positions: they are simply how I felt at the time, and I think there is a certain value in the recording of them for others to read.

For the sake of establishing some sort of minimal pattern, I have re-arranged the 'entries' in my notebook to form separate chapters, the subjects of which I think will be self-evident.

'If it's not a rude question, what *do* you want us for?'
'For research — what other purpose is there?'
From *Eagle* (children's comic)
etc.
□

The report has several characteristic reporting modes. One is the diary/commentary arising from observations:

□ *Friday, 4 March*   At 1.30 p.m. we assemble for the first stint. I know room TA4 well. Most colleges seem to have pockets of 'temporary accommodation', and as it happens, this one has become permanent. A prefabricated hut isn't the most relaxing of places, and this one's thin walls and proximity to the main road mean that noise is something of a problem. An estate agent would call it 'light and airy', I suppose. Students clatter across the floor and settle into the rows of canvas chairs, ones with awkward wooden peninsulas for resting note-pads on. Whenever I've used them, they've had a life of their own. There are fourteen students — one missing. My practised tutor's eyes note there is only one male amongst them — has anyone researched into the problems of the lonely male in college literature classes? — an older female student at the back looking organized and purposeful, and the usual isolated girl on the front row (why?). I place a bet with myself that these two latter ones will be 'talkers'. I win the bet. A.Y. enters, carrying a sheaf of duplicated poems, and two books — one very slim, which turns out to be a reproduction of an early, hand-printed Auden collection, and a big, expensive *Collected Poems*. The progress of a poet in two volumes. No lecture notes: he doesn't use them. This does wonders for student morale, but not for mine, as I always feel undressed without notes in a lecture-room. Later, the students tell me how much they appreciate a tutor who isn't glued to a text: tidy desk means tidy, full mind.

Casual, no fuss start: neither a bang, nor a whimper. A.Y. spends the first fifty minutes explaining the course aims and administrative matters. Assessment will be by examination at the end of the course. We will be doing the two poets in turn, not concurrently. Suggests the class divides for part of the sessions into three groups for discussion purposes: 'syndicates', he calls them, and my mind drifts off to Eliot Ness and Kojak snuffing out the mafia bosses. Sessions will be tripartite: report-backs from the groups, 'input' from A.Y., and then discussion sessions at the end of the afternoon. I make a mental note that, last thing on Friday afternoon, students' minds are going to be on other things.

2.20 p.m. Eyes down to Auden-Larkin. A.Y. asks, 'Why Auden and Larkin together?' Well, both have been enormously influential and important poets. Auden dominated the 1930s, though his influence fell away later. Similarly Larkin in the 1950s. 'Poets who set a style — the style for their times,' and then were challenged by succeeding generations. There are 'poetic, critical, even political aspects' to their work.

etc.   □

The second is a free-ranging critique of the view of education offered by the college's CNAA-validated course submission:

□ *Student discovering themselves and the world*   I take it as axiomatic that the college student — whatever else he is doing — is finding out who he is, and exploring the standards that he and others live by. If this is so, it seems to me that, in shaping our syllabuses, we have to start from where the student is at when he arrives amongst us, and see his college education as an act of growing.

A corollary of this must surely be that we should never view whatever 'skills' or 'knowledge' he acquires in simply neutral or objective terms. I would plead for a recognition that it is a limitation in a college's work to see 'values' only in terms of a student's efficient functioning as a learner and as a future teacher, and I fear that there are certain disturbing echoes of this way of thinking in today's talk of 'professionalism' and 'accountability' in education. Whilst thinking about this, I came across the college CNAA submission's list of six 'dispositions and attitudes' considered appropriate for the intending teacher:

The student

1 Is conscious of, committed to and responsible in his membership of an education profession;
2 Is conscious of his responsibility to and for society;
3 Is committed to education as a continuous process;
4 Is concerned for and committed to children;

5 Is confident as learner and teacher;
6 Is self-aware, self-critical, imaginative and rational.

I would probably want to make a case out for each of those points taken individually, but as a total statement, they seem to me inadequate in that they don't correspond to most people's experience of being either a teacher or a student: in some ways, they are six prescriptions for the ideal civil servant, rather than the kind of real-life teacher pointed to in the following: 'It is very difficult to feel at ease in the classroom, to spend five hours with young people, and not emerge wiped out or exhausted at the end of the day.' (Herbert Kohl)
etc. ☐

The third characteristic reporting mode is the transcript-with-commentary. In this example the evaluator reflects on a student discussion which the lecturer has set up and then withdrawn from:

☐ 'I can see one irony, to start off with, and that is the fact that, although he's perhaps somewhat critical, at the same time he still seems to have a certain amount of reverence for the place.'

(*J.C.* A tentative hypothesis that gets near to the pulse of the poem. Less directive than would be a similar opening by the teacher, it is an invitation, an appeal.)

'I don't think he is so much giving his personal point of view, as sort of a general point of view . . . what, you know, might happen to the church . . . I don't think he's showing his lack of reverence for it.'

(*J.C.* The students have probably settled on the key phrase, 'awkward reverence'. The modification forces the first student to justify his opinion.)

'I don't think this is how everybody reacts, though, when they go into a church, do they? This is only *one* type of person's reaction.'

'Well what is the reaction?'

(*J.C.* Again, the challenge forces the student to develop his point. This is interrogation between equals — perhaps ultimately more fruitful than that between teacher and students?)

'Well, I'd say that it's a mixture of reverence, the reason being he can't quite understand, and a sort of dislike, the reason being. . . . Perhaps that's what the poem revolves around — the fact that it's all a bit of a mystery . . . why the church is there in the first place?'

(*J.C.* Alas, he's floundering. So the next student bales him out.)

'I think he's saying the church doesn't have as much value as . . . doesn't mean as much to many people as it did at one time, and he's wondering if this will end when the church will become something that people don't really know what it is . . . they go in to read the gravestones, or to . . .
etc.   □

Fourthly, the evaluator offers a random collage of student responses to the course on which he neither provides commentary nor imposes structure, leaving interpretation entirely to the reader.

□ 'I would have preferred the course to be longer so that each of the poets could have been dealt with in more detail — Auden in particular; in this way the course would have been more beneficial in that the students would become more familiar with, and also more positively critical of, the poet's work.'

'I found that the course as a whole required a good deal of concentration.'

'The two poets I found difficult to relate to one another at times, though the lectures did clarify to a small degree some of their similarities. I would have preferred to spend more time on this aspect of the course.'

'Like many of the courses I have attended at Charlesford I felt at the end of the course that I would have liked to have spent more time to study the books, poems, themes and so on in more detail.'

'I felt that in the course many questions were thrown out which still remain unanswered for me personally. I would prefer a slightly more positive approach.'

'I felt the course was far too short to be able to do justice to the two poets studied. I was just getting interested in Auden — his work and ideas — when we had to switch to Larkin. When I had finished the Auden section I felt I had learnt very little and certainly not enough to feel confident to take an exam.'

'The relationship between the two poets was clear, but perhaps it could have been established at the beginning of the course.'

'I hadn't studied any poetry by Auden or Larkin before. At first I didn't particularly enjoy them but as I reached the conclusion that both are pessimistic poets and accepted this I find I enjoy and understand them more.'

etc.
□

Fifthly, the evaluator transcribes sections of what he is careful to avoid terming an 'interview', since he argues that this is too constraining:

□ *A conversation*

The interactions between people can never be reduced to a tidy pattern. What started out as an interview became a conversation, but with the interviewer (myself) holding back and conscious of his role, one minute, and then loosening up the talk into something more fluid, the next. □

This 'conversation' is in effect a debate between colleagues on the teaching of English in teacher education courses in which the evaluator offers no claim to interviewer neutrality.

□ *J.C.* So you would say, I think, that as a literature teacher, one has to be conscious of the fact that one's students are not just studying an academic subject but they are going to go out into the world, they're going to become teachers. Some of them are going to become English teachers, others are going to become teachers of other subjects. I notice, for instance, in your lectures you quite frequently refer to the sort of problems one meets in the classroom.

A.Y. Yes. Mind you, I would take exactly the same line, as I do with my college students, if I were teaching an extra-mural class. I would say, it isn't so much teachers as they all become people . . .

J.C. People?! . . . (*J.C.* I'm obviously happy to see A.Y. come round to a point of view I favour!)

A.Y. Persons. These happen to be also teaching persons.

J.C. You can't be a very good teacher unless you are a fully-developed person? (*J.C.* Are we ever? I think we are both getting a bit fuzzy, here.)

A.Y. It's the *person*, rather than the teacher, I'm interested in. I also throw out some . . . I suppose you'd call them 'tips', if you like, but that's a bit narrow for what they are because they are going to become teachers. I think the view that people can't be many things at once is one you find quite a lot nowadays. I believe people can take things at many levels at the same time. I'm teaching a person, who is also going to be a teacher, who is also mad on literature (I hope!).

J.C. Are you as happy teaching the novel and drama, as you are teaching poetry? I ask this question because you have a sort of 'prat. crit.' approach — these two words that neither of us can pronounce — and poetry lends itself, more than the other two genres, to the practical criticism approach.

A.Y. Yes. I think this is true. I tend to use this approach, even if I'm studying drama or the novel. I tend to take a small part. . . . Yes, I'm just as happy. I once went to a lecture by Harry Levin, and he was discussing just this problem, and he thought 'prat. crit.' is an often much-abused phrase — I abuse it myself, actually. I can see what he meant when he suggested that what happens when we are studying the great works — say, *King Lear* or *War and Peace* — is that one can start anywhere in the book, and you can start with a very fine piece of — when I say 'fine', I mean in the eighteenth century sense — a very fine piece of analysis, and then you work out into all the dimensions of the book, and if that's 'prat. crit.', then it's different from what I think people often mean by the encapsulated, tiny piece cut off.   □

This engaged, interventive stance is clearly a long way removed from conventional evaluator roles; so much so that it tends not to be considered even in the context of discussions about the relative merits of internal and external evaluators which concentrate on the issue of 'contamination' versus 'knowledgeability', or on what seems a mainly spurious distinction between the insider's 'subjectivity' and the outsider's 'detachment'.

The merits or otherwise of this style of evaluation deserve debate and the extracts above may help to stimulate this and to provide a partial exemplification of the notions of educational 'criticism'/'connoisseurship' offered as alternatives to conventional evaluation by Eisner (1979). However, the Charlesford portrayal study was undertaken in 1976–7, on a deliberately exploratory and tentative basis, before the 'curriculum criticism' idea had emerged as a distinctive strand in educational evaluation. Although what we have here is engaged critique, grounded in close observation and personal, committed response, it does not make the claims attributed by Gibson (1981) to advocates like Eisner, Willis, Walker, Mann and Jenkins. It does not rest on a view of curriculum as art object, or of this type of curriculum evaluation as methodologically grounded in principles of artistic and literary criticism; Gibson's reservations about such studies need to be noted. The relative attractiveness of their reporting language (by comparison with that of conventional evaluation reports) can seduce the reader into a too-easy acceptance of the judgements. The effectiveness and productivity of the approach depend to a greater extent on the personal knowledge and skills of the evaluator than do more conventional approaches, where the methodology can have a degree of independence from its user and thus may more readily satisfy objectivity criteria — a piloted questionnaire or interview schedule, for example, or a standardized test or scale. The open invitation to subjective response and readability may in extreme cases lead to a self-indulgence of language and opinion; the domination of the personality of the evaluator rather than the object of the evaluation. Like journalism such accounts are not necessarily based on an integral methodology: their impact may be high but their construct validity and reliability difficult to demonstrate. At its best such an approach offers deep insight, at its worst, the writing can be a long way removed from the standards of critical seriousness claimed as its touchstone. Yet the applicability of Gibson's criticisms depends not only on reporting style, but on methodological issues and especially on the sorts of claims made for the outcomes or 'findings' of such an exercise and the uses to which these are put.

Are they to provide generalized 'information for decision-makers' of the sort that the original student routes data offered? Or to encourage and support professional development — something the student routes data offered no real potential for, but this study does in abundance? In furtherance of the latter goal, it is also worth arguing, studies like the present one or the Professional Studies evaluation described earlier are doubly productive: here the actual evaluation *process* has at least as much potential for promoting professional development and institutional theorizing as the evaluation *product* (i.e. the report), while the only process gains from the routes study were to the evaluator's computational and analytical skills.

Among the various reactions to this unconventional style of evaluation that of the lecturer concerned is of most interest, for the report, which was available throughout the college in the usual way, offered a critique of his pedagogical style, and the assumptions about knowledge and learning on which it was based, which was more detailed and uncompromising than in any other study. (It must be mentioned that the report went to this lecturer in the first instance and would not have been published without his agreement.) His response revealed a radically different perception of the role of evaluation and of the validity of evaluation 'findings' from that of the B.Ed. committee whose reactions to studies have been cited previously:

☐ I believe that a forthright and creative critic . . . is a very stimulating presence in any class situation, and this stimulation works on both the lecturer and the student. . . . (The mode of evaluation) is subjective. This is not in itself a bad thing, but such 'evaluation' can never come to an end. One would wish to challenge many of (the evaluator's) own assumptions about literature and . . . a very interesting dialogue could take place. . . . Maybe the benefit of the experience is to be found in stimulating creative self-criticism amongst teaching staff. . . . I believe the experiment was worth trying . . . and I think other subject areas may find that it has the positive results I have outlined.   ☐

To the B.Ed. committee a critical statement in an evaluation report constituted a threat which had to be neutralized; the classic device for neutralizing unpalatable evaluation findings is to reject them on the grounds of weak methodology. Critical and threatening though the portrayal evaluation might have seemed, to the lecturer concerned it presented no such problems: it was simply more grist to the mill of constant critical self-appraisal and in a sense a bland supportive report would constituted a betrayal of that process.

Many explanations can be proffered for this difference in response (compare for example, the quotation above with the reactions of the B.Ed. committee to the previous two studies). Some of them have to do with individuals' security within their professional roles. A.Y. was an experienced teacher who clearly gained deep personal fulfilment from the collective, critical exploration of literature. The course committee, whatever its members' individual qualities as teachers, was a body with little experience and knowledge of the task of course management; its posture was primarily defensive. A related difference here was in the 'theorizing' commitment of individuals and groups. The lecturer welcomed any stimulus to professional development and the concomitant assumption that there is always room for improvement, while the committee needed the reassurance (provided by a 'successful' study like that of students' routes) that it was operating at the optimum level of efficiency. But hypotheses like these do not fully explain such divergent responses as we have illustrated and we suggest that perhaps more fundamental is a difference in perceptions of the purpose and status of evaluation findings and conclusions. The B.Ed. committee required information for administrative decision-making and received such findings as if they ought to be, or claimed to be, final 'truths' about the educational process. A.Y. was concerned with the appraisal and refinement of pedagogy and with his own professional development and treated the portrayal evaluator's judgements as no more final than his own. In this he may have been helped by the fact that the reporting style of the portrayal study was manifestly debatable and contentious while the language of evaluation reports is usually — and deliberately — of a studied neutrality and finality. But is the report grounded in questionnaire or semantic differential scale data less debatable intrinsically than the impressionistic study grounded in close observation and dialogue? Perhaps what needs most to be identified is the apparent naïvety about the truth claims of evaluation reports: the most any evaluation, whatever its methodology, can provide is *evidence offered in pursuit of the truth*. Despite this, evaluation evidence is frequently treated as the terminal point in the evaluation process, as providing or claiming to provide 'proof' of a course's quality or success, whereas it can only constitute a stage in a more or less continuous educational debate. The expectation of proof and conclusiveness, the quasi-scientific view of educational evaluation, is deeply rooted and ultimately inimical to the process of educational development.

In as much as this course's managers required uncontentious fact and its teachers material for debate and development, we wonder how far these very different expectations of the role of evaluation reflect adequate models of educational management. Is it really legitimate for the management of educational activities to exclude the qualitative, theorizing, dimension? We shall treat this issue in greater depth in chapter 5).

Note

1 The scale of the Professional Studies evaluation can be summarized as follows:

Participants

students: 322
lecturers: 33
teachers in associated schools: 40 responded to questionnaires and a further 60 (approx.) attended meetings

Instruments and procedures

1 questionnaire to students
1 schedule to lecturers
2 questionnaires to teachers in associated schools
7 meetings between lecturers and teachers in associated schools
Numerous lecturing team meetings to discuss interim reports

Reports

3 preliminary analyses of student questionnaire data
3 analyses of lecturer schedule data
2 analyses of serving teacher data
7 reports on meetings with serving teachers
1 final report on the entire Professional Studies evaluation programme
1 summary report for the academic board
1 summary report for students
1 summary report for serving teachers
1 summary report on action taken in the light of evaluation

EVALUATION IN PRACTICE
AT ENLANDS

Samples from the Enlands evaluation

In chapter 2 we mentioned that the Enlands research project 'A Study of Student Choice in the Context of Institutional Change' was devised by senior management, in consultation with the DES, to collect data about the criteria by which students had chosen the colleges, their courses and the students' level of satisfaction with these courses.

'Institutional change' provided a context within the title rather than one for the research. Institutional 'self-study' during the research was assumed to be the province of senior management. Through most of the duration of the project the DES, through the steering committee, required statistics in a form that could be interpreted by their planning and statistics branch. With this range of expectations of the project, dealing with three institutions which, for the most part, had not made preparations either for the collection of statistics or for institutional self-study, squeezed out for much of the time the opportunity to engage in evaluation. Yet the combination of 'institutional change' and 'self-study' with the stated intentions of the project to conduct a 'responsive' evaluation, seemed to signal that collaborative research could be pursued on issues identified by any staff, assisted by the evaluation agent. Some of the responses to these offers of collaboration were described in chapter 2.

The examples of evaluation process and reports in this chapter were begun in response to issues that were selected more by the researchers than by staff or students. These evaluations were not conducted within an agreed set of procedures that had been publicly agreed by the institution. Indeed, few staff sought such curriculum evaluation. As such, these examples do not represent self-evaluation which is premised on at least an awareness of a mutuality of issues by a group of staff. Action research may develop this awareness and lead to self-evaluation but it was collaboration as a research methodology incorporating self-evaluation (Schensul, 1980; Fletcher and Adelman, 1981) that this author (Adelman) aspired to develop.

Certainly at the beginning of the project the institution had 'extended the hand of welcome' and offered co-operation in the work of the project. But these expressions of welcome and openness to the institution were conditional on the assumption that the project would not inquire into areas of contention. The consequence of engagement in evaluation was not personal hostility but the institutional equivalent, ignoring the process altogether. We emphasize in this book the need for institutions to prepare agreed procedures for the conduct of evaluation that take into account pre-conditions of history, organization, management and accountability relationships and not to treat evaluation merely as technical assistance in information provision.

The three examples of evaluation that follow were conducted during the research project. They were not required work requested by senior management or by the steering committee, but were in response to expressions of concern by some staff and some students which connected with information that had been gathered through regular questionnaires to, and interviews with, students. These questionnaires and interviews were, as we have noted, part of the formally agreed project. These three examples and the fourth, which derives from subsequent development of institutional self-evaluation of courses and programmes, were concerned with aspects of the curriculum.

Example 1   Book loans and 'personal' education

During interviews, students in the cohort at Enlands mentioned the lack of time to read outside the areas specified by their assignments. As the college had claimed that the B.Ed. fostered 'personal' education, particularly during the first two years, and that subjects could be studied in breadth as well as depth, the apparent lack of reading, even by students of English and History, outside their areas of study, seemed contrary to this claimed quality of the degree. To find out the extent to which the student interview cohort was reading beyond what was needed for the assignments, a systematic collection of book return slips was arranged with the library. During the following eleven weeks, the researchers collected all the slips for books returned to the library. From these slips were extracted those books borrowed by the members of the cohort. A note was made of the extent of matching between the content of the book and of the course unit being studied by the student. The analysis of this data showed that few students were reading outside the areas of their courses and that books were being returned in sets related to the topics of assignments. New sets of books would then be borrowed. The total of the students' reading could not be known only from library loans, nor were the library loans the only books used to complete assignments. For the most part, the students made notes from books in the library and returned to their residences to write the essays.

Borrowing a book from the library was a commitment to a particular interest or concern. The analysis also showed that the greater the frequency of loan of books, the more likely it was that students achieved higher grades in their assignments. The findings of this study of library loans indicated that the students, whatever their subjects of study, were constrained by the nine-unit structure of the degree and the frequency of the unit assignments into limited patterns of reading. The student cohort, in follow-up interviews, said that they did not consider that there was time to follow up personal interests that had emerged from the courses. The library study suggested that the claim that the nine-unit structure embodied the fostering of personal education, particularly during the first two years, could not be taken at face value.

As with many of the studies completed during the project, audiences within the colleges were not specified nor obliged to respond. The findings of this study were reported to the librarians and subsequently to the discussion group within the college. The librarians were interested to see that the frequency of returns had peaks and troughs (which corresponded to assignments being completed) as this corroborated their impression of being extremely busy dealing with some courses followed by a period of some quiescence. As the library tended to be under-staffed in relation to the peak times, this organizational aspect of the findings was seen as most pertinent. The educational implications of the study, as comment on the course's claims in respect of personal education, were not pursued at that time, despite the fact that personal education followed by professional preparation was a corner-stone of the college's rationale for the nine unit-structure.

Two years later in the submission of the second revised B.Ed. it was acknowledged in the section on evaluation of the previous B.Ed. that there was clear evidence that this approach (the nine units per annum for years 1 and 2) had resulted in a level of fragmentation in study and overloading of assessment which was unacceptable. 'Whatever their own schedule an investigation of library loans showed that books which students took out of the library were narrowly restricted to the assignment they were undertaking at the time.' Amongst other changes the revised B.Ed. reduced to a maximum of six the number of courses that students would take in any year.

This library study provided data which was not used as evidence until the institution had revised its perspective on the educational worth of the B.Ed. programme of study. The development of this fresh perspective involved prolonged, heart-searching discussion within committees, staff conferences and in the usual informal ways. At the time of the research project there was a need to maintain the credibility of the B.Ed., given that the survival of this and other colleges depended upon the recruitment of students. Bad news did not go far within the college and was certainly not intended for conveyance outside. The version of the library study that was reported to the steering committee contained information only on the frequency of the loans and the correlations with grades achieved and age and sex of the students. Had the library a computer-assisted record of loans and returns, the study would have been easy and light on manpower. As it was, the clerical work involved in the sorting was so time-consuming that the continuation of the study as such, although suggested by some members of the steering committee, was resisted by the researchers.

Example 2   The teaching practice year — an evaluation of students' satisfaction with staff support and contact.

The first two years of the B.Ed. were largely concerned with personal education; the first opportunity that students had to engage in teaching practice came in the third year of the degree. Prior interviews with the student cohort and reports from staff suggested that many students were anxious about their ability to cope with their teaching practice and about the adequacy of the preparation for this practice and its relation to the previous two years of study. These issues had emerged quite early in the study. The senior research fellow had asked the advice of the committee concerned with Professional Studies as to the potentially most useful procedures and topics for this study of the teaching practice year. The committee members were asked by the chairman to express their views. Each of them avoided encouraging such a study. Objections were raised on technical grounds, such as the extent to which such a study could reliably represent the experience of students on the three age bands (first, junior/middle, secondary), the appropriateness of the methodology that might be employed and the fact that the degree was validated and could not be amended. The chairman told the senior research fellow, 'You are the researcher, you do the research.' Such a response goes against any aspirations to conduct a responsive evaluation where the issues of concern to practitioners are made the centres of inquiry by the researcher. The study of the professional year was held in abeyance but the issue was raised again the following year by some tutors responsible for the supervision of students in the third year. The tutors cited the complaints of some students about lack of adequate supervision and pointed to the need for an evaluation that would ascertain whether those complaining were typical of the students as a whole.

The researchers began listing the issues that had arisen out of teaching practice and its connections to the B.Ed. as a whole. In the form of questions, this list was sent to some tutors to check on accuracy, relevance, coverage and terminology. Some amendments were made and the emergent questionnaire was sent to all third-year students towards the end of their teaching practice period. Distribution of the questionnaires was through pigeon holes: a procedure found to be lacking in effect. It was also towards the end of the term and near examination time. Only 35 per cent of the students returned the questionnaires. However, there were sufficient students in each of the age bands, of each sex and 'mature', as compared to those who entered college straight from school, to make it worthwhile to report the findings.

The senior research fellow was following the suggestion of the committee from the previous year, that as the researcher he should find ways of doing the research. No negotiations about procedures or clearance or the way in which the study would be reported and to whom were conducted. The findings of the study were sent to the heads of the three age bands and to the director of Professional Studies. A note attached to the findings offered further copies on request and suggested a meeting between the senior research fellow and each of the sets of age-band tutors.

The findings were favourable to one of the age bands, whose group took up the offer and requested a meeting and copies for each of the tutors. Another age-band group, for whom the results were equivocal, requested further copies and eventually agreed to a meeting, whilst the third of the age-band groups requested neither copies nor a meeting. The meeting of the first of the age-band groups was cordial and the staff attested to the credibility of the findings in spite of the low return. They said they could learn much from the evaluation that would be valuable to them in their revision of the professional practice supervision. The meeting with the second set of tutors was initially marked by considerable suspicion and expressions of disdain towards the findings and the low return. The representativeness of the findings was questioned. Some of the comments that the tutors considered to be unfavourable were actually equivocal or even favourable. At this point the leader of the set of tutors suggested that the senior research fellow discussed the findings point by point. When the exposition had been completed, there was noticeable relaxation in the posture of the staff and inquiries were made for further elucidation. Some staff suggested that the findings were credible and should be taken as criticisms that should lead to adjustments in the supervision in the future.

Evaluation reports are often difficult for recipients to deal with rationally. Implications are read into reports, particularly by people who have high standards and are diligent in their work. It is often tutors who feel most anxious to succeed who are most upset by any apparent criticisms of their adequacy. Comments from the third group were made in passing, and these comments were about the low return and thus what was considered to be the non-representativeness of the replies.

No decisions that related explicitly to this evaluation were taken but teaching practice located solely in the third year was removed from the revised B.Ed., and as the evaluation report submitted to the CNAA by the college in 1980 put it:

☐ The theory/practice link needs to be made more explicit for the majority of students and in this connection most students would like to have experience in the school earlier than year 3. The evaluation, however, did not lead the college to the conclusion that it should revert to a concurrent style although not surprisingly this did have its advocates . . .

The evaluations show small self-directing syndicates[1] to be particularly effective at primary level although the importance of specific subjects at secondary level has made the impact of the syndicate less significant here. However, the evaluation also indicates that the heavy demand that this syndicate system places upon a small number of tutors is unacceptable and modifications which reduce the intensity of this burden are necessary for the future. The evaluation further led the college to the view that the pertinence of the theory/practice connection was also related to the nature and quality of the supervision and school experience.   □

This example indicates that all feedback should be accompanied by subsequent discussion of any documents to ensure that misunderstandings and misinterpretations have not occurred either as a consequence of inadequate expression in the feedback document or through misreading or miscomprehension.

Example 3   The provision of reading and literacy courses within the college

This case study was begun in July 1977. It attempted to describe for the benefit of staff at Enlands some of the issues involved in the provision of the reading curriculum. The case study began with an introduction.

□ *Introduction*

It is hoped that the reader, as a member of the college, will individually and in the course of discussion with colleagues recognize or come to realize other aspects that impinge on these issues. The documentation that has been drawn upon has been mentioned in the text. The key interview was with the tutor of 2027, after which the inquiry sheet was circulated to all those current members of the college who have been involved in teaching and making decisions about courses in reading and literacy. Subsequently some of the staff were interviewed to cross check the information already collected. I realize that some of these issues are already matters of debate and to an extent are being considered along with the development of a new academic structure. It is hoped that no one mentioned will take this document as more than an attempt to be specific about procedures and organization impinging on the teaching of reading. This case study is intended to feed discussions about academic structure and teacher preparation.

The provision of reading and literacy courses within the college

Thirty-nine fourth-year B.Ed. students will be taking the unit
H/2027 as one of their two advanced professional courses. Twenty-
six are intending first school teachers, ten middle school, and three
secondary school. Amongst the other twenty-nine advanced
professional courses listed in the catalogue distributed on 16 December 1976, H/2027 is described thus:

> The course is designed for students who wish to develop, beyond
> the basic level, their interest in reading so that they may make a
> special contribution to the selection of media and techniques and
> the development of policy within schools.
>
> In the light of recent research it will examine in depth both the
> 'normal' learners and those with special problems and ways of
> assisting them fruitfully.

An earlier (21 June 1977) list of student selection of fourth-year
courses showed forty-three students as having chosen H/2027. Of
all the fourth-year courses, H/2027 is the one in greatest demand
and this was envisaged as being the case.

The introduction to the catalogue of advanced professional
courses (16 December 1976) states:

> While the categories of unit overlap, all attempt to utilize and
> integrate knowledge and understanding gained in the first two
> years and the professional experience of the third.

After the publication of the initial professional course selection I
began to wonder:

(a) how one tutor would be able to deal with the requirements of
    forty-three students taking a unit at honours level of duration
    one year;
(b) how many of the students were building on second- and third-
    year work;
(c) how many of the students were intending to teach in secondary
    schools.

Question (a) was put to the tutor in charge of H/2027 . . .

She recalls that she was studying for a doctorate in reading and
language arts whilst on exchange to a university in the USA during
the time when the B.Ed. degree was devised and submitted to the
CNAA. Two units dealing with aspects of reading were eventually

approved. These are 'The development of literacy', which was devised by two tutors who left the college before the first intake of students, and 'Language: an analytical approach', which includes an option for students enabling one term's study of linguistics related to reading. The tutor in charge of H/2027 has always taught the optional segment of 'Language: an analytical approach', which is available as a course unit. There are also courses in aspects of reading during the third year, but these are for students intending to teach in first and junior/middle age bands.

One of the consequences of allowing students to choose their courses (even within the constraints of focus, timetable and rules for mutual inclusion and exclusion) is that there is a considerable variation in formal knowledge of aspects of reading. There is no free-standing unit on aspects of reading available to all B.Ed. students prior to the fourth year, although the 'The development of literacy' unit is available as a course unit in the second year. This availability was provided after requests from some students in 1975. This variation may be expressed as a table:

Reading and literacy courses previously taken by the current H/2027 students

		Student type						
Year		A	B	C	D	E	F	G
1974–5	1	Language: an analytical approach	–	–	–	–	–	–
	2	Development of literacy	√	√	–	–	–	–
	3	First or junior middle	√	Sec.	√	Sec.	Sec.	√
1977–8	4	2027	√	–	√	√	–	–
		0	8	0	28	3	?	?

The 'The development of literacy' course is described thus:

The concept of literacy and its place in contemporary society will be examined and an analysis made of the reading process, the variables involved and relevant research findings, together with a study of the teaching of reading.

It is selected in the second year by some B.Ed. students as one from a set of three options, the other two being 'Children with special needs' and 'Methods of educational inquiry'. The course leader says, 'About 40 per cent of the students take the "The development of literacy" as an elective unit.' In answer to question 1 on the inquiry sheet the course leader replies, 'The second-year course is about the psychological *processes* of *literacy* — not how to *teach* reading. Therefore there should be only limited overlap.' Interviewed later, he elaborated on these points:

> I wouldn't think for one minute that any student who's com-
> pleted that second-year unit is in any position to go into school
> and teach reading as such. I would think there are lots of things
> that they're certainly not aware of at all. For example, I would
> think that one of the things they were unable to do would be to
> analyse various reading schemes and so on, and establish criteria
> for selection in relation to particular children, and so on, which is
> a fairly crucial one here in the professional area. It depends on
> what their previous knowledge is, what their previous focus is
> and what is their selection of units, and so on. I would suspect
> and hope that people who have done that unit in the second year
> are more aware of the problems and certainly have got, what shall
> we say, conceptual knowledge that they can apply and probably,
> hopefully, will pick up the skills all the more quickly.

The tutor of 2027 returned from the States at the time of the submission of the course of which she was a nominal member. After the course was referred back to the college by the CNAA the tutor, along with the co-ordinator of the first school course, asked the former course leader if the unit 'The development of literacy' could be rewritten with the third year and the fourth year[2] in mind. It was suggested that as the course might not be validated the 'Develop-ment of literacy' unit might be deleted from the submission if there were problems with its content. The CNAA made no comment on the 'development of literacy' unit when it was resubmitted and approved as part of the course. Eventually (1975–6) 70–80 students opted for 'The development of literacy'. The co-ordinator of the first school course and the tutor for H/2027 declined the teaching of

'The development of literacy'. They considered that, although it had CNAA approval, its content was not appropriate for second-year students. Coincidentally, an American professor of reading and language arts was on a study exchange. He agreed to a request made by the dean of Educational Studies to teach the five or six groups that had opted for 'The development of literacy'.

The two who had declined to teach this unit suggested later in the year[3] that a staff development course taught by the American professor would be useful, to prepare staff within the college for the teaching of this and other courses on reading. This suggestion met with approval from the dean of Educational Studies, the dean of Professional Studies and the principal. However, such a course did not transpire, perhaps because the professor taught the 'Development of literacy' groups five days a week and had some post graduate classes. The tutor in charge of H/2027 volunteered to teach one group taking 'The development of literacy' in order to relieve the teaching load of the professor.

When the American professor left in May, the dean of Educational Studies maintained that the tutor in charge of H/2027 was responsible for the teaching of the 'development of literacy' unit and accountable for the fulfilment of the validation conditions. The tutor considered that she was not responsible as she had neither devised the unit nor had effected through her representations any revision of the unit. The 'development of literacy' unit was handed over to the present leader of the junior/middle school course in reading who took five of the groups, the tutor in charge of 2027 continuing with the sixth.

The part-time tutor received a copy of the syllabus, made minor adjustments to facilitate her teaching and enable a small amount of practical work with remedial children either in school or in college to take place. She comments, 'One of the snags with the third year we are finding is that quite a lot of the ground (covered in the 'development of literacy' unit) is covered again from a slightly different angle, which is perhaps a disadvantage.' In 1976 she had requested that the third-year reading groups be separated into those who had done 'The development of literacy' and those who had not. 'But, you see, I only teach junior/middle anyway, so I asked for the junior/middle ones; but this wasn't possible because of the way in which they choose their syndicates. This would seem to me the logical thing to do, to have them able to go on to something fresh, as it were, in the third year; but I don't think it's really practical.'

In the third year, first-school age-band students have nine weeks of various courses in the first term and then go out for four weeks' teaching practice, during which time they are asked to collect recordings of children reading on tape. The students return for four weeks at college during which time they analyse the recordings and deal with questions arising from their analysis of these recordings. Students then return to the college for two more weeks and complete the year with more teaching practice.

The co-ordinator of the first school course's answer to question 1 includes, 'The second year is basic, intended to pave the way for advanced studies by laying the foundation.' However, of the thirty-nine students taking H/2027, only eight took 'The development of literacy' in year 2 and six of these are intending first-school teachers.

In order to compensate for the different levels of knowledge and expertise, the tutor responsible for 2027 divided students into four groups according to the age bands in which they intended to teach. She maintained that the four groups — 5–7, 7–9, 9–11 and over 11 — would be appropriate because of the different sorts of skills that need to be developed in these age bands and a mixture in terms of middle- and secondary-school reading requirements. She distributed a form on which students listed the relevant courses already taken, three books that they had read on reading, and any area of interest they particularly wished to develop. She included the latter to accommodate any gaps in knowledge which students considered they required, for instance students who had taken the middle-school course in the third year, but claimed they knew little about phonics, and others who were interested in remedial reading. The tutor had selected schools appropriate to these perceived needs.

To deter those of the initial forty-three who were not fully committed to taking the unit, the tutor proposed a heavier assessment than any of the other twenty-eight advanced professional units. She required eight assignments, one long essay of the 'dissertation' type and an exam. The tutor's attention was drawn to these assessment demands by the dean of Professional Studies. The tutor requested that the requirements be temporarily retained to deter those whose commitment was not strong. Before the end of the summer term 1977 the dean of Professional Studies formally brought the assessment requirements of the unit into line with those required by the CNAA. However, a few students were deterred and the assessment requirements, although conforming with CNAA regulations, are considered to be relatively heavy compared to other fourth-year units.

Subsequently some students have been excluded by an assessment regulation that states that a maximum of two courses with an 80 (course-work)/20 (exam) pattern may be taken in the fourth year. If students have already made firm selection of two such courses, they would not be able to take H/2027 which also has an 80/20 pattern, but would instead have to take courses with a 60 (coursework)/40 (exam) pattern.

All the respondents to the inquiry sheet agreed that students got sufficient opportunity to discuss their fourth-year courses with syndicate tutors (who are also academic counsellors for third-year students) and, where appropriate, with fourth-year tutors. The students are said to have discussed their choices 'very sensibly' and showed understanding of the implications of their choices. Two respondents gave some details in reply to question 12. Estimates of the number of staff who were capable of teaching the fourth-year unit 2027 ranged from two to five. Respondents suggest that students opt for 2027, (a) because primary teachers see the course as essential, and (b) the word has gone round that students who took a dissertation or maxi-option on reading were amongst the earliest to get jobs. No one asserted that all twenty-nine of the advanced professional units were equally important as preparation for teaching careers.

Comments

I perceive the following issues that might be worth discussion within the College.

1 The conflicting requirements of teacher preparation alongside the attempt to maintain autonomous choice of curriculum for students.

1.1 It may be difficult to justify 'The development of literacy' as personal education. The distinction between personal and professional does not seem to be clear-cut in this and some other first- and second-year units.

2   What is the relationship between the third- and fourth-year studies in reading? The majority of the students taking the fourth-year unit have only done the third-year courses.

3   That a unit-based course arrangement requires consultation and negotiation that are difficult to provide through the work of committees or by idiosyncratic decisions.

4   The possible need for a systematic monitoring of students' programme profile.

5   Overlapping in course content is not only a symptom of the reticence to discuss curriculum content without the barriers of status and rank, but also of the absence of organization by the CNAA for overviewing the total programme. Fourth-year units were devised subsequent to the rest of the programme and have been validated in isolation. Segments have tended to be validated in isolation from one another in the past.

6   In terms of professional roles, a course arrangement that is complex and interdependent may necessitate a precise distinction between the responsibilities of a role and to whom a role-encumbent is accountable.

7   To what extent can it be said that students who have not taken preliminary courses in reading and literacy have sufficient foundation for embarking on what are honours-year professional courses?

8   Is it appropriate that one tutor should be responsible for thirty-nine varied students during an honours-year course? Might the tutor's workload be considered too heavy to give individual students sufficient attention?

The inquiry sheet

Would you please reply to these questions. Your replies will help complete a case study about the fourth-year reading unit.

1   Do the second-year courses in reading overlap with those of the fourth-year advanced professional units?

2   Are you surprised at the number of students selecting the Reading unit in the fourth year?

3   Do they have to have completed the second-year courses as pre-requisite to taking the fourth-year unit?

4 How many of them have taken second-year courses?

5 How many people in the college could, workload permitting, teach the fourth-year reading unit?

6 Do you think the reading unit in the fourth-year should be restricted to intending primary- and middle-school teachers?

7 Were students advised, for instance by their academic counsellors, about their fourth-year professional units? Who does give advice?

8 Are all twenty-nine of the advanced professional units equally important as preparation for teaching careers?

9 Do you think the students have enough information and experience at the end of the third year to make an appropriate choice from the professional units?

10 Why have they tended to choose reading then?

11 Do you consider the courses in reading to be intellectually challenging enough to be at honours level?

12 What does the fourth-year unit in Reading entail for the student? □

The case study of literacy was begun with some trepidation about the reaction of staff that might become involved. The staff were defensive, aggressive but never compliant or complacent. This, as with the other examples, indicates the responsiveness of the institutions' members to *specific* issues involving a limited part of the institution. Reports on an institution as a whole or on the three institutions were responded to only by those few with a perspective or knowledge of institutional policy and planning or those with a knowledge of the issues of debate within the DES, CNAA, and the public sector of higher education.

Although the beginning of the subsequent meeting of the discussion group which considered the literacy case study concentrated on the methodology and validity, discussion did eventually move round to what the study indicated about the college's strategies for curriculum development. The case study, then, achieved what many of the other project documents which had been released for discussion had not achieved. The college members did not avoid relating the document to their own practice. After the discussion, which the group said it had found very worthwhile, the chairman suggested that the case study be available to others in the college. There were no formal channels through which to release the case study. About a year later, few members of the discussion group could recall even the gist of that meeting.

How the evaluation information was applied

These examples may seem to indicate that even research and evaluation that tries to address the issues of practitioners and policy-makers has little take-up (Cohen and Garet, 1975; Rein, 1976).

The underpreparation of the colleges for the presence of the project, particularly the absence of formally constituted groups of staff to read and respond to evaluation reports, precluded them from exploring the applicability of the evaluation reports. Even when the colleges became familiar with the project and the discussion groups had been set up, there was a time lapse of about three to six months before the pertinence of the research documents was appreciated. Where research information was used to inform decisions on college policy and programmes, this process took even longer. The feedback of research and evaluation reports preceded any development by as long as one year, even when the colleges had established procedures for the receipt and discussion of project reports. Where particular staff acted as gatekeepers, controlling the release of project documents within the institution, the pertinence of the project's work could not be appraised by other, even senior, staff.

The three colleges had established discussion groups, by different means, with different representatives, and had adopted different extents of control over the release of project information to the college staff. By the end of the project, even at the college where the principal had demonstrated considerable interest and support, had convened a widely representative discussion group, and had incorporated findings and extracts from project reports into college and public documents, he attested to the long time that elapsed before the relevance of the project's documents was appreciated. In contrast, in the college where the project's work was considered to be a threat to its reputation there was, even by the end of the project, no indication of any application of the research findings. In this college the discussion group comprising the senior management acted as gatekeeper for project information.

Enlands college, at which the researchers were based, began to use some of the information from the project as evidence to CNAA of having evaluated its programmes. But it was after the project had concluded in 1979 that the project's work was drawn on in the development of new programmes of study.

Part of the evaluation process involved regular attendance by the researcher at meetings of some of the college committees, particularly those concerned with courses. Towards the end of the first year the researcher was sometimes asked by the chairman to comment on a point that had been raised. The researcher's response was that as a non-member of the college and as independent researcher, he had no right to comment on the deliberations or decisions of the college or its committees. These attempts to draw the researcher into discussions were not always spoken. Sometimes a nod or wink was intended to indicate, 'You and I have this understanding, don't we?'

Although the researcher did not intervene on his own initiative, he was on one occasion tempted enough to acquiesce to an invitation to comment in a decision-making forum. The occasion was a meeting of the academic board (which the evaluator had regularly observed) towards the end of the project. The topic was the desirability of retaining student choice. A number of project documents released to the college had dealt with the idea and actuality of student choice, but little discussion of this aspect of the curriculum had taken place. The researcher took up the invitation to speak as an opportunity to display the relevance of the project's work to the issue under discussion.

The researcher's avoidance of an advocate's role on controversial issues reduced the immediate impact of the project's work; the institution was more accustomed to forthright expression of opinion. However, there were other barriers to the take-up of the project information. The following occasion indicates the role of the gatekeepers.

At a meeting of Enlands' staff, the researcher was asked to talk about the progress of the research. The level of interest of staff seemed high and some questions ensued. Mention was made of the interim report and staff were invited to ask for copies. Towards the end of the meeting the college linkman said that there were too few copies of the interim report to be freely available, although there were more than fifty copies spare. Fewer staff than expected asked for the interim report.

The ways in which the project information was considered and used at Bellnova College was markedly different from those in Enlands, reflecting differences particularly in the accountability relationships. At Bellnova the principal engaged in discussions of the project, included references and extracts in his papers, encouraged the widest dissemination of project information. The research and evaluation information which emerged was quite favourable to the college and its practices. Where indications of inadequacy were clear, as with the prospectus information, discussion and action took place quite promptly. Extracts from the evaluator's report were used in the re-submission to the validating university and in several public lectures given by the principal.

Development of procedures for the conduct of institutional evaluation within Enlands, (1979–81)

Under the terms of its original approval, the CNAA required Enlands to provide evidence, after five years, that the programmes had been critically scrutinized. Until 1979, the evidence that was usually put forward to the CNAA consisted of external examiners' reports and impressionistic accounts of what students, staff and (in the case of the B.Ed.) schools considered to be the strengths and weaknesses of programmes.

In 1979, the CNAA published *Developments in Partnership in Validation*. Although the term 'evaluation' was not used, the document referred to the ability of the institution to provide a 'self-analysis' that went beyond registry statistics, formal structures and resources, and external examiners' reports.

External examiners spend relatively little time in institutions and although they may talk to staff and students and see some of the students' work, they do not have adequate or extensive information about the course or its relation to the programme, or of its consequences for the students to be able to make more comments that extend out from their function as assessors. The function of assessment is not co-extant with that of evaluation.

The CNAA document implied that these 'self-analysis' accounts would be taken as indicative that the institution had had a clear idea of its policy and was capable of monitoring its programmes. These accounts would be indicative of what the CNAA view as the 'health of the institution'. The Enlands senior research fellow had stated, in his new role as research co-ordinator, that in 1979 he would continue to encourage and foster the development of a means of evaluation of courses and programmes within the institution. *Developments in*

Partnership (CNAA, 1979a) provided the lever to shift opinion at Enlands towards the need to encourage systematic evaluation.

The research co-ordinator presented a paper about the CNAA *Partnership* document to the research committee, who recommended that it go forward to be discussed by the development committee responsible for planning and monitoring courses and curriculum. The paper was noted but not discussed.

The B.A. programme was beginning its fourth year of operation; at the end of year 5 the programme would be re-submitted to the CNAA. The programme director invited the research co-ordinator to discuss ways in which the programme might be evaluated. About the same time, in the summer of 1979, a second revised B.Ed. was about to be planned.

No formal statements about evaluation were offered to or discussed by any committees at this stage. The initiative for beginning discussions about evaluation came from the research co-ordinator as an interpretation of the significance of the CNAA document *Developments in Partnership in Validation*. A year later, the CNAA sent a document entitled *Institutional Reviews: Notes for Guidance of Institutions* (1980), to all institutions it validates. This document was intended to clarify what sort of documentation the CNAA required as evidence for institutional 'self-analysis'.

The research co-ordinator believed that *Developments in Partnership in Validation* prompted Enlands to pay attention to the need for evaluation. Enlands, like most other institutions, Charlesford being a notable exception, would otherwise have been slow to introduce evaluation of courses and programmes across the whole college. Approval of courses and programmes in the initial validation and the comments of the external examiners would have sufficed as indications that the courses were up to standard.

Example 4 The development of procedures for the evaluation of the B.A. programme and its courses at Enlands

The research co-ordinator suggested, in continuing discussions with the B.A. programme director, that issues which emerged from the operation of the programme should be identified by those involved in the managing of the programme and teaching its courses. The notion of 'issue' was not familiar to staff as used in this sense. A definition was provided: 'An issue is a real or apparent discrepancy between aspiration and practice.' In this case the aspiration was expressed in the programme structure as outlined in the submission and the experiences of the practices of the programme. It had already been agreed that the issues arising from the programme would be dealt with separately from issues arising from courses. Discussion about evaluation with two course leaders commenced about this time and the suggestion that the course team identify issues was made by the research co-ordinator.

The idea that practitioners' (in this case, teachers') issues should form the agenda for the evaluation was expounded and used by Stake (1976) and developed during the Ford Teaching Project (Elliot and Adelman, 1976). In the context of higher education this idea had been in use since 1974 at Charlesford and for some time in some American universities (Braskamp, 1980). The idea is straightforward: that practitioners have most knowledge (both propositional and tacit) about the practices of teaching, their assessment and course content. Rather than impose an evaluation whose issues are derived through assumptions made by the evaluator often working on behalf of the senior management or bureaucracy, responsive evaluation puts the onus for defining the human situation on practitioners. The aspiration of responsive evaluation is to foster self-evaluation through a process of self-accounting. But issues raised by tutors may not be recognized or seem significant to students. Through questionnaires and interviews with students, not only is the relevance of the issues identified by staff ascertained, but the transformation of the issue into a question provides information which tutors begin to use as evidence in their judgements of the worth of their own practices as delimited by the courses. Thus both the mutual recognition of an issue by those that study the significance of the issue and the students' view on the issue are collected and the onus is then on the staff to make connections between these aspects and to make judgements of worth of present practice and suggestions for revision.

Following from discussion between the programme director and the research co-ordinator, six issues were drafted to be considered by the programme committee for their relevance and significance. The programme committee, with wide membership, included all those who taught on the courses and student representatives from all the courses. The first meeting to discuss these issues was held in the summer of 1979. The six issues were, with some amendments, agreed as being significant and worthy of evaluation. The research co-ordinator formulated a set of questions which asked the students to express their experience of the programme issues as these affected their courses. These questions were drafted in the form of a questionnaire.

The terminology and syntax of the questions and the adequacy of the questionnaire as drafted were discussed by the programme committee, some amendments were made and the questionnaire was then distributed to all third-year students engaged on the programme. Distribution was through tutors to their individual classes; the tutors collected the questionnaires at the end of class. The return was 85 per cent but was slow to come back as tutors administered the questionnaire over a period of three weeks. Students were not required to append their names to the questionnaires, only a note of their new major or minor courses of study was required. The returns were processed by computer. A report was prepared by the research co-ordinator which gave the numbers and percentages of replies in each of the three categories over all the programme, then broke them down into replies from each course. By putting the replies into a positive, or neutral, or negative, category, an overall 'total' could be given which would indicate the weighting towards the positive or neutral or negative. As it was the operation of the programme as a whole that was being evaluated, this aggregation seemed to be pertinent. The draft of the report was discussed with the programme director to check that it was comprehensible. Some amendments were made and copies provided for all members of the programme committee.

The committee met and, as one of the items on its agenda, members discussed the report. The programme director kept close control over the discussion in that he went through each of the six issues and gave his interpretation of what evidence the questionnaire provided regarding the issue and then invited members of the committee to add their comments and interpretations. The discussion was concerted and constructive. No decisions about changes in the programme were made at the meeting. The questionnaire and its findings were a preliminary to a slightly revised questionnaire in the following year. This was administered directly through the offices of the research co-ordinator to each student group, the tutors having agreed to this during a programme committee meeting. The minutes of the programme committee meetings were distributed to all staff teaching on the B.A. There was no reason for any B.A. staff to claim that they did not know of developments in the evaluation.

The returns for the second programme questionnaire were in the region of 90 per cent. A similar analysis was made utilizing the computer facilities and a report was written using the positive, neutral, negative, notion. A whole meeting of the programme committee was devoted to discussion of the report and its implication for the programme. At this meeting it was agreed that particular amendments would be recommended to the CNAA in the re-submission of the programme. Staff attention was drawn to particular aspects of the programme's operation. The programme director requested staff to be more diligent in their feedback of comments on students' work.

The procedure for the evaluation of the programme, the issues identified, the form of the evidence that was collected but not the substance and the recommendations for amendments in the programme, were embodied in a report to the CNAA, written by the programme director and approved by the programme committee.

The evaluation of courses was separate from the evaluation of programme. Confidentiality, insulations were suggested as necessary between course teams unless the course team wished for a mutual exchange, for instance, offering reciprocal interviewing services with another course team. Three course teams engaged in evaluation in 1979–80. In 1980–81 all the courses engaged in evaluation. The majority formulated issues in the way suggested by the research co-ordinator and then discussed the appropriateness of questions that would shed light on these issues. In all cases in order to preclude identification of students, the questionnaires were returned to the research co-ordinator's office for typing and collation and when requested, analysis.

The procedures followed were:

1 Tutors meet as a total group to identify their concerns about a course or course component. These concerns are developed into a list of issues.

2 The list of issues is given to an agent of the evaluation for reformulation into questions. The more specific the issue, the greater the matching between single questions and single issues.

3 The questions are constructed to avoid taking it for granted that the issue raised by staff will be recognized by the students. The sequence of questions tends to progress from the more general to the specific.

4 The students are interviewed separately. Their replies are trans-

cribed; answers to each of the questions are collated to preclude identification of the student. The collated replies are presented to tutors. Tutors discuss the extent of discrepancy between the issues identified by them and those identified by the student.

5 Tutors as a group pick out the evidence for discrepancy between aspiration and practice, and spontaneously make connections between these realizations, their initial meeting (where they sought to identify issues), and their feelings of unease and success that they held prior to the evaluation.

These procedures are based on the following premises:

(a) Those responsible for designing and teaching a course have to take major responsibility for its consequences, both intended and unintended, for students.

(b) The student's experience of a course consists of the sum of the various components he has taken and which have been taught by a number of tutors, i.e. his particular programme. Thus it is the responsibility of the group of tutors teaching the course to take joint responsibility for the outcomes of the course and their teaching.

(c) A corollary of (b) is that no individual teacher can be held wholly responsible for inadequacies of the course. (There are obvious exceptions, such as absence for some reason or other. Even in such a case, however, it could be argued that it is the responsibility of the other tutors to compensate for such absence.)

(d) Systematic and rational collection of information about the students' experience of the course will necessarily be attended to by tutors if the questions that the students are asked are derived directly from issues that the tutors have raised.

(e) Discussion amongst tutors based upon eliciting students' experience of the course can be used by staff to make judgements about worth, that is, evaluate the course content, structure and its pedagogy.

(f) Placing responsibility for evaluation upon those who teach the courses ensures that discussion is informed rather than based upon opinion, impression and prejudice. This is not to say that these latter will not flavour the discussions leading to the judgements of worth, but if statements are required to be supported by evidence, then the relationship between such statements and this evidence will have to be made publicly explicit. By requiring that the staff jointly raise issues to be transformed into questions for the students, consider the students' responses and take joint responsibility for these as consequences of the course, one precludes to a large extent the victimization of individual staff and fosters a more supportive relationship.

Where the issues that had been identified were concerned with interconnections within the course, for instance details of pedagogy in relation to course content, the students were required to recount their experience in detail. The research co-ordinator requested in such cases that students be interviewed. Apart from two courses where students were interviewed by mutual agreement between tutors of the two course teams, these interviews were conducted by the research co-ordinator, transcribed and typed by the research assistant and secretary. The students' replies to each of the questions were collated and the interviewees' questions and interventions were deleted. The student replies were sent to the course team in this form. Although in 1979 one of the course teams had found the variety of student response so extensive that it asked the research co-ordinator to write a report on the student replies, by the second year this same course team were able to make their own analysis of the student replies.

Some staff suggested that these evaluation procedures were too student-centred, but these were not staff who had engaged in course evaluation. Comments from those engaged in these procedures for evaluation attested to the usefulness and usability of this information. By this time the CNAA *Institutional Reviews: Notes for Guidance of Institutions* (CNAA, 1980) had been published. These suggested that evaluation reports describe the procedures adopted, and specify how programmes and courses might be revised. The substance of student replies and staff discussions would not be required. As a pilot attempt to write a report on this basis one of the teams that had engaged in evaluation in each of the two years wrote a report which was read by CNAA officers and was strongly approved of. The programme director sent this report to course leaders as an example of what was required by the CNAA. Course leaders wrote reports using the format and these, along with the programme evaluation report, were forwarded to the CNAA as evidence of the college's ability to evaluate its programmes and courses. Extracts from the geography course evaluation are included for the purposes of illustration.

□ *Course appraisal*

During the last four years staff have given much attention to the content, teaching and co-ordination of their units. These discussions have been taken into account in the modifications proposed in this review. A more formal evaluation of the course took place in the summer of 1980 and the results have also been included. Mr Clem Adelman, the college research co-ordinator, acted as evaluation agent. The following procedure was adopted:

1 The course team identified possible discrepancies between the aspirations and practice within the course.
2 After discussion with Mr Adelman these issues were turned into a number of questions. Mr Adelman then interviewed each final-year student and, in addition to responding to all the staff questions, each student was invited to comment freely on any other aspect of the course.
3 The responses were taped, and a typed transcript of all the responses was drawn up by Mr Adelman and presented in such a way that it was not possible to identify the replies of individual students.
4 The transcript was studied for indications of possible strengths and weaknesses in the course. The results of this analysis have been included in this review, each member of the course team taking the evaluation into account when considering the revision of his or her unit.

The course team was encouraged by the number and range of favourable responses in the evaluation report, which indicated that in general the course has met its original aims and objectives. A second evaluation, carried out in the summer of 1981, was based on an amended questionnaire with more precise questions. This yielded fuller information about student reaction to the course and the responses supported the findings of the previous year. Modifications related to the earlier evaluation were shown to be appropriate. The process of evaluation is helping us to build on what appear to be the strengths of the course and to remedy weaknesses perceived by the students and the course team. The modifications have been prompted by the results of student response of the course and by discussions within the course team about academic developments within the field of regional development study since 1976.

The considerations have led to decisions which point to the retention of the existing rationale and framework of the course but envisage adjustments to the content of some of the units in it. In particular, we have taken steps to integrate the first-year fieldwork more closely with other work of years 1 and 2. We have improved the quality of the first-year economics course and strengthened and analytical skills elements of years 1 and 2. Our external examiner has given strong support to these proposed modifications.

Summary of proposed modifications

(Of the twelve items, four have been included in this extract)

Year 1 Introduction to economics The revised course will have closer relevance to current economic problems facing Britain and there will be more emphasis on relationships between economic philosophies and the processes of economic development. The revised unit should provide a stronger base for understanding the world economic order and for the study of regional development issues at second-year level. The changes proposed reflect student and staff views about the limitations of the original unit.

Year 1 Introduction to regional studies Course evaluation suggested that students were insufficiently aware of the first-year Easter field course and its role in the whole programme. Accordingly, this unit will make much more use of examples and illustrations drawn from the field study region (South Wales) and students will be given a clearer introduction to the field course.

Year 2 Third World development issues Little change is proposed in this unit. However, we suggest that theories and models of economic development should be introduced at an earlier stage and that more emphasis is given to alternative approaches to the problems of eliminating poverty. The other modifications relate to the inclusion of material on new ways of improving frameworks for trade and development. Again, these proposed changes reflect shifts in academic concern since the mid 1970s.

Year 3 Political geography Modifications are proposed in order to clarify the relationship between this unit and the rest of the

Major. The adjustments will place more emphasis on the ways in which territorial organization affects the economic capacities and development problems of states. There will also be more emphasis on the developmental aspects of international groupings and organizations. □

On the basis of the information collected through this process of evaluation, informed judgements can be made as to what action to take in amending or replacing curriculum components. The information collected through the evaluation process may, but often does not, have a simple direct relationship with the action that is eventually taken. For instance, a percentage response on a questionnaire that indicates a 60:40 split amongst students on that particular item does not necessarily mean that the tutors should adjust the curriculum to meet the positive or negative response of the majority. Other concerns have to be taken into account and these ordinarily include the relationship between that item and the rest of the curriculum, the institutional pre-conditions and the constituency of the students. Informed judgements are made on the basis of an understanding of interrelationships and interactions within the curriculum. To treat percentage questionnaire responses in the manner of an opinion poll does not indicate such an understanding of the interrelationships within the curriculum or the circumstances of the institution. Acknowledgement of this distinction between the process of evaluation and the judgements based on information coming from the evaluation report and taking into account these contexts means that any decisions may take some time before they can be implemented.

Meanwhile, the second revision of the B.Ed. was approved by the CNAA. The programme director of the B.Ed. had begun discussions with the research co-ordinator about procedures for evaluation of the B.Ed. The programme director of the B.A. attended these discussions. A document on evaluation was offered to the B.Ed. steering committee as the procedures for the conduct of the evaluation of the B.Ed. These means were approved.

The research co-ordinator met members of the B.Ed. scheme design group to discuss the purpose and procedures for evaluation. Some objections from members of the committee were received. One suggested that the evaluation would become too prominent and an 'industry' in its own right. The B.Ed. group suggested that the research co-ordinator should write a brief paper about evaluating courses and programmes to go forward to the courses committee.

The courses committee discussed this paper and approved it as an outline of the means by which the college would allocate responsibilities for course and programme evaluation. Further discussion of the paper ensued at academic council (an open forum for all staff). The paper was accepted as the way in which evaluation would be conducted within the college.

By consultation and prolonged discussion with the programme director and course leaders, by further discussions at committee level and by personal discussions with individual members of staff, procedures for evaluation of courses and programmes were devised and given approval by the staff of the college. No discussions were held with senior management about the relationship between course and programme evaluation and reports of the institution's evaluation of its own practices and structure. Here lies a dilemma. The course and programme evaluation has been accepted as necessary and valuable both for the process of the re-submission of programmes and courses and for instrinsic value as a means to improve the educational worth of the courses. However, it still has to be seen how the educational and academic concerns of courses and programme evaluation will articulate with the institutional aims and policy as defined in the account that will be written by the senior management. There are bound to be discrepancies between these two sets of accounts and it remains to be seen whether the CNAA appreciates the inevitable consequences of their own emphasis in validation over the years on efficient management and control of resources as the *sine qua non* of a 'healthy institution'.

The nature of these developments in institutional evaluation were informed both by the preceding research project's attempts to foster self-study and by the comparisons between the process in the two colleges that the authors of the present book had begun to talk about.

Using the *evaluation decisions* as analytic categories, the reader will recognize that Enlands recent developments include decisions about goals, focus, organization, dissemination and, to a considerable extent, application. Decisions about methods and criteria would be made according to the focus and goals of the particular evaluation, as in the case of the B.A. and its courses.

Notes

1 A group of students, with one member of staff, who discuss their experience on teaching practice during that year.

2 The CNAA initially validated the first three years of the B.Ed., fourth-year courses being devised little by little subsequently.

3 A similar suggestion had been made at the beginning of the year but no action had been taken.

5

EVALUATION AND EDUCATIONAL DECISION-MAKING

The two approaches to institutional evaluation described in the preceding chapters were independently conceived and implemented and they highlight rather different issues of significance to those concerned with evaluation. The Enlands project crystallizes problems of the appointed evaluation agent's roles and relationships, exacerbated when such an appointment is from outside the institution. The comparison with Charlesford underlines this point. At Enlands it took several years for the initial aspirations of the evaluation agent for a relatively open and responsive form of evaluation to be realized, while at Charlesford the agent had the advantage of having worked for several years in the institution as both teacher and course manager — roles to which the notion of 'evaluation' implied the strongest threat — and he was therefore able to anticipate many of the problems and to ensure that the ethical and procedural character of the evaluation was firmly enshrined in a 'constitution' formally ratified by the institution's academic board.

At Enlands, the challenging character of the emerging evaluation findings tended, initially, to provoke resistance to the responsive evaluation procedures. At Charlesford, the commitment to openness, shared control and plurality of perspective was made by the institution in inevitable ignorance of its possible consequences. Had the college already experienced evaluation of the kind outlined in chapter 3 before that commitment was made, it is possible that course management bodies at least would have resisted vesting control of evaluation in an independent body and coupling this control with a policy of open dissemination. At Charlesford, therefore, the 'problems' emerged only after the programme began to deliver contentious insights and findings which served increasingly to demonstrate a basic lack of congruence between the interests and imperatives of course management and course evaluation. At Enlands, early consciousness of this lack of congruence impeded the conduct of the evaluation from the outset so that it took several years of sometimes difficult negotiation before the Enlands evaluation achieved a position roughly comparable to that of Charlesford and even then a major factor was external — the CNAA self-appraisal requirement (which was only vague rhetoric when the Charlesford constitution was agreed).

Clearly, then, the juxtaposition of Enlands and Charlesford must serve to emphasize the absolute necessity for institutional evaluation being subject to clear and negotiated ethical and procedural principles, grounded in thorough institutional analysis. Moreover, since such analysis requires the sort of familiarity with the complexities of the institution's culture which comes from engagement with it over a period of time, the outsider brought in specifically to engage in evaluation or evaluative research (as at Enlands) is at a clear disadvantage in respect of securing those grounded preconditions on which the success of an evaluation programme depend. This disadvantage might be sufficient to outweigh any advantage of 'detachment', lack of 'contamination'/'vested interest' (see Hoste, 1975) which an outsider might offer if it prevents the job being done properly: in institutional self-evaluation, unlike academic research, methodological questions are meaningless unless coupled with the power to influence events. In any case, as the Charlesford programme showed, an institution is perfectly capable of securing for itself, if it wishes, an approach to evaluation which incorporates elements of both outsider detachment and insider insight, while also minimizing or at least balancing the effect of group and individual interests.

We now discuss the dimensions of such necessary institutional analysis. The key here lies in 'institutional'. It does not matter that the activity may be called '*course* evaluation' (or 'course monitoring'): if it takes place in an institutional context it becomes to some extent evaluation of teachers and to a very considerable extent evaluation of the institution itself. What is revealed by the Enland and Charlesford evaluations is not only the adequacy or otherwise of the new courses and programmes but the adequacy of the institutions' ways of organizing themselves to cope with change, and to promote educational and professional development on the basis of systematic appraisal of their work.

In at least two senses, all evaluations are 'political', firstly, in that an evaluation involves acts of valuing, of making judgements of worth or effectiveness, and this presupposes the existence of other, no doubt competing, values and judgements. In an institutional evaluation these will be to an extent politically located, and certainly, if some judgements prevail over others in the decision-making process, the judgements will have consequences for the distribution of resources and the status of individuals and groups. Evaluation probes and exposes the character of educational enterprises which are institutionally-located and managed. These enterprises are framed by organizational structures and decision-making processes on the one hand, and the interests and sensitivities of individuals and groups on the other. Any evaluation, in such a context, offers a critique of and a potential threat to these processes and interests and to the balance of institutional power. Secondly, an evaluation can be political by intention in that it can be used by one group to secure or maintain its interests, to promote or prevent change in power relationships.

What an evaluation can do, therefore — and undoubtedly what it did at Enlands and Charlesford — is to act as a particularly powerful means of making the political realities of the institution explicit to the groups and individuals involved. Concomitantly, what the experience of institutional evaluation — and the increasing demand for it — must produce, is a far greater attention to the institutional context of evaluation, and a relative redressing of the balance away from the obsession with arguments about methods and techniques which dominated evaluation writing in the 1960s and 1970s, and for many is still seen as the major, or only, evaluation 'problem'. Institutions developing evaluation programmes need to work out the roles and relationships of those central components of institutional decision-making to which evaluation necessarily relates in organizational terms and to which, as we have suggested, it provides a critical response and possibly a threat. These central components are (a) the means for educational management in general, and (b) the means for educational and course innovation in particular.

Congruence and consistency: rhetoric and reality

The ideal relationship between evaluation, academic management and educational innovation is, of course, one of harmony and mutual support. In neither Enlands or Charlesford did this symbiotic state always obtain.

The present chapter is concerned in part with the question of why this should be — why, for example, the evaluation committee and the B.Ed. course committee at Charlesford came increasingly into conflict as the evaluation programme developed, to the detriment of genuine educational advance; and why Enlands was unable to fulfil its aspirations to engage in self-study. Since formal evaluation was in a sense the interloper or latecomer it seems reasonable to suggest that the conflict reflected weaknesses in the evaluation process. This is far too simplistic. Rather, evaluation forced into the open underlying tensions and conflicts, and raised questions about the reality of the basic concepts on which academic life in such institutions claims to rest — 'rationality', 'democracy', 'professionalism', 'the pursuit of excellence', 'the furtherance of knowledge'. Evaluation identified inconsistencies and incongruences between the practice and conceptual basis of the three strands of educational management, educational innovation, and evaluation, each of which in various ways is premised on these 'basic concepts'. The message then would seem clear — if you can achieve consistency/congruence and cohesion between the strands then the way to institutional improvement is open.

But our experience showed a deeper and more pervasive inconsistency between what people say and what people do, between the 'rhetoric' of management, innovation and evaluation and the 'reality' of each, or between their 'espoused theory' and their 'theory in action'. For at the level of the claims made for these activities there was no inconsistency. The Charlesford evaluation programme, for example, was democratic, pluralist, participatory — but then so, since the Weaver Report (DES, 1966), was the mechanism for academic management, with its academic board, its various committees and the careful balance of interests represented on these bodies. The evaluation constitution simply extended the Weaver principles into a new field. For this reason, whatever people's private qualms, nobody had a public case for voting against the evaluation proposals in the academic board, and nobody did.

So congruence at the level of formal procedures is not sufficient; what is also necessary is consistency between the outward, formal structure and style of each strand, and the efforts of those who operate it; between the rhetoric of management, or evaluation, or innovation, and the way each is enacted; between the rhetoric of one, and the reality of another in a context where they are related and mutually dependent.

We can argue that as far as the two evaluations were concerned there was a fairly high degree of internal consistency in this regard: the deepest inconsistencies lay in the area of educational management. It is our view that if institutions really wish genuinely to use evaluation as a means of improving the quality of their educational endeavours they need to give most attention not to evaluation pro-grammes as such but to the overall frameworks and processes of management: if these are adequately reflexive, responsive, self-regenerating and decisive at all levels (assuming educational manage-ment to be something engaged in at various points in an educational institution, right down to day-to-day planning for teaching), then there is probably less need to embark on an additional programme of formal evaluation. What we have termed the 'theorizing institution' (c.f. the use at school level of the phrase 'the thinking school') imbues *all* its day-to-day decision-making processes, not merely those at the classroom level, with reflection not only on action but also, and initially, on the educational need and justification for actions of particular sorts. The institution which most suggests a failure in this regard, paradoxically, is not the one which has no formal evaluation programme, but the one which does — which hives evaluation off into a distinct compartment. 'You're the evaluator, you tell us how good a course it is,' is a shrugging-off of the responsibility for that critical reflection which is absolutely fundamental to the rhetoric of 'professional' conduct.

We need to look therefore at this broader framework of academic management and decision-making, and to consider in what ways and to what extent it is able to promote and accommodate edu-cational evaluation, whether the process of evaluation be formally organized and specialized in the responsibility of evaluators and evaluation units/committees as at Enlands and Charlesford, or undertaken as part of the staffs' everyday individual and collective commitment.

'Democracy' in higher education institutions

As is appropriate in a society whose leaders make frequent claims to defend democracy and individual liberty, institutions such as Enlands and Charlesford had an overt commitment to democracy in their internal decision-making. The Weaver Report on college government (DES, 1966) led to the setting up of a form of internal government where an academic board could provide a fully-representative forum for debate, restricting a principal's power to act autocratically. Academic boards were usually serviced by a number of committees and at both board and committee levels membership was a combina-tion of *ex-officio*, constituency elected, and co-opted. For many colleges this did indeed represent a genuine democratization of decision-making: a move away from the autocratic, sometimes whimsically tyrannical rule of principals over staff and students alike in some colleges and the *laissez-faire*, easy-going approach in others. Both Enlands and Charlesford were in the forefront of the move to implement the Weaver recommendations.

However, as Lynch (1979) points out, this style of government was subjected to increasing strain in the years following the James Report on teacher education (DES, 1972a). It could just about accommodate the relatively restricted range of decision-making entailed in a period of expansion, affluence and university validation, especially since the latter condition pre-empted many of the most significant educational decisions which needed to be taken. But to cope with the decline in student numbers, with mergers, re-development, redundancies and an unprecedented programme of course development, new infra-structures were needed. For those colleges like Enlands and Charlesford which transferred to CNAA validation, a major new area of decision-making and collective responsibility had to be accommodated. This concerned, for the first time, whole educational programmes — the rationale, structure, content and organization of courses, from initial planning to validation and implementation — as opposed to the mere teaching of courses devised elsewhere.

The models for this extension of decision-making already existed in some polytechnics and other LEA-maintained institutions validated by CNAA, with their centralized control, matrix management structures and networks of committees and officers. Both Enlands and Charlesford, like many other colleges of education/higher education, evolved highly complex structures (to the extent that at Enlands the CNAA suggested that they had gone too far and their structure was more suited to a polytechnic with 7000 students than a college with 1400). This was done in a very short space of time, often with minimal debate. The new structures were serviced by a new breed of professional administrators: previously senior academics frequently took on the major administrative responsibilities in the way that they still do in some Oxbridge colleges. By now (1982) some of the former colleges of education are frequently very similar structurally to the polytechnics, though their smaller size has enabled them to preserve something of the old college of education congeniality. Now, it would be untrue to assert that the colleges prior to reorganization where more 'democratic' than they are now. Indeed, in many the Weaver reforms went only skin-deep, and complacent, compliant or soporific academic boards ensured the continued dominance of autocratic principals and heads of department. Moreover, of course, questions can always be asked about the particular forms of democratic government practised: on decisions taken, for instance, on the basis of the typically British first-past-the-post voting system which in theory can produce a 'minority' just a fraction of a per cent smaller than the 'majority'.

The chief problem for the democratic claim in such institutions is what to do about dissent — not always as substantial as the 49·9 per cent minority vote necessarily, but nevertheless present in the difficult post-James period to an extent not revealed by the consensus rhetoric of majority rule democracy: 'It was the view of the college that . . .'; 'The feeling of the meeting was that . .'. Backed by a complex set of standing orders an academic board or major committee decision taken on the basis of majority votes, however slender, could not readily be reversed, and — of particular consequence for the evaluation process — a succession of crucial decisions about the future direction of colleges and courses could produce a cumulative legacy of alienation and disenchantment. The problem here was that decisions had to be taken, and the majority vote seemed the only way to resolve disagreement. But once a decision was taken in this way, dissenters were expected to accept and implement it on the basis of 'collective responsibility' and while this may be practicable within the sort of relatively straightforward policy matters that pre-James academic boards had been used to, it was not so easy where the major value issues involved in large-scale course planning were concerned. For what this approach to some extent denies is the reality, the inevitability, of pluralism in British educational institutions: education is nothing if not value-laden. Yet the complexity and depth of the value issues involved (in this case relating to how best to train teachers of children growing up in the latter part of the twentieth century) tended to be suppressed, and the process of 'enforced consensus' could in effect become an imperative for institutions seeking CNAA validation, for that body insists on staff cohesiveness. The dissenter in such circumstances would no longer be tolerated as someone merely having a different viewpoint but could be seen as threatening the very survival of the institution and its staff, for during this period failure to gain validation could indeed affect the security of the institution itself, such was the pressure colleges were under. Loyalty to the institution was infinitely more important than commitment to deeply-held principles about the educational process, and such loyalty was defined, simply and pragmatically, as acquiescence in the views of the institution's leaders.

It is possible that at the root of these difficulties was a failure to grapple with the notion of 'democracy' itself and a consequent assumption that institutional democracy could have only one outward form. In the same way that Raymond Williams (1976) detects sharply divergent meanings of the word at the level of arguments about the relationship of the individual to the state, so two comparable senses of democracy are detectable in recent higher education. Williams contrasts democracy as *popular power in the majority interest* with liberal *representative democracy* conditional upon open elections and freedom of speech. The operational mode of democracy in these institutions is — nominally at least — representative rather than populist. But it is complicated, and in some cases we suspect it is negated, by management actions and procedures inconsistent with the underlying ideology, and by the fact that only a limited proportion of those responsible for college government are elected. Formal bodies always combine *ex-officio* with elected membership, and it is important to understand that in many colleges in the period after James, key posts in connection with course development and management were filled by appointment, not election, and by internal appointment which was rarely subject to the publicly agreed conditions and safeguards which usually operate where external open competitive appointments are made.

Decision-making, management and innovation

The democratic claim was maintained in institutions like Enlands and Charlesford throughout the period in question, and is maintained at the present time. This claim is a constant: what changed was the mode of operationalization of the claim. Both colleges moved from a fairly simple hierarchical structure to a more complex one; both became more bureaucratized in their processes; and in both, for the first time, models of institutional management were applied which are now very familiar in all parts of higher education, but especially in the LEA maintained sector. We need to explore now the characteristics of these processes as they were applied to the course renewal, and to consider the appropriateness of the model for educational institutions in general and for educational change in a period of continuing instability in particular.

Both institutions evolved increasingly *bureaucratic* forms of organization in their search for the most efficient way of coping with the escalating challenges of the 1970s. In Weber's terms (1964) bureaucratic organizations reflect a legal-rational mode of authority (consistent in the present cases with the decline of charismatic or traditional 'principal power' after Weaver). There is a critical dependence on a clear demarcation of responsibilities, the obligation to abide by rules, the assumption that offices are filled by the people having the most appropriate 'technical' expertise and knowledge and the overriding assumption of consensus over institutional goals. The objective is efficiency in working towards the achievement of these goals. At Enlands and Charlesford the bureaucratization was manifested in an elaboration of the committee structure and a considerable expansion in the number of new specialist roles — directors of courses, of course development, co-ordinators of segments of courses, of assessment, of forward planning, (and even research co-ordinators and advisers on evaluation!). Where previously the individual academic's professional role encompassed a wide range of interrelated tasks, these were rapidly pared down to the basic task of teaching, while, as the other side of the coin, the individuals fulfilling the newly-created posts, who were also academics, were often relieved of all or part of their teaching duties in order to undertake their new responsibilities. Thus, to quote from a 1973 management paper at Enlands (our italics):

> The new organization will represent a major change of emphasis in the work of the head of department, since *he will lose all direct responsibility for the admission and progress of students.* . . . His responsibilities will be much more firmly rooted in the subject discipline, since he will be spokesman for the collective wisdom of the staff group under his leadership.

A very similar paring down of head of departmental responsibility occurred, in the same year and in response to the same perceptions of need, at Charlesford: the rhetoric of 'collective wisdom' does not disguise the scale of the shift in institutional power away from departments towards the newly-appointed course/programme administrators. At the time, this process of fragmentation, delegation and specialization in relation to institutional roles seemed the logical response to the increasing diversity and complexity of the institutions' functions, especially once they started out on the road to CNAA validation.

However, the process has important consequences which are exacerbated by the application of the model to *educational* institutions. As Selznick points out (1949), delegation and increased role specialization lead to a divergence of interests within the institution, and to an increase in the likelihood of conflict between role incumbents and groups. The 'matrix' structure adopted at both Charlesford and Enlands, with its two axes of course teaching and course/institutional management, produced just this conflict not merely at the level of power in the college's decision-making arena, but in a more fundamental way between the traditional academic values of departments and the new imperatives of efficient course planning and management, in which styles of thought and action were applied across the board to achieve consistency in course proposals without regard to their consistency with the rather different educational world-views of, say, teachers of literature and teachers of mathematics. And, as Selznick also points out, the divergence of interests and the increase in intra-institutional conflict necessitates a parallel growth in the need for attention to matters of strategy. This point was rapidly perceived, and the key technical skill demonstrated by many incumbents of the new roles tended to be political. Educational planning is, in theory, about aims, objectives, rationales and so on; in practice it was about persuasion, manipulation, compromise, the art of the possible rather than, necessarily, the art of the educationally desirable. The final form of the Charlesford B.Ed. well illustrates the outcomes of this process. The stated rationale, loyally defended by all staff to the CNAA, highlights liberal education, processes of inquiry and the unity of theory and practice. To achieve this, structural changes were needed within the institution which politically were unachievable, and the reality of the course in action reflected the compromises which had to be made: a traditional 'content' rather than 'process' orientation, and a continuance of the notorious divide in teacher education of the gulf (as perceived by students) between theoretical perspectives and practical action in schools, which was guaranteed because 'theory' and 'practice' continued to be taught by staff in different departments.

The institutional tension produced by these structural changes, and by the shifts in power and much more explicit politicization of institutional discourse, was exacerbated by the growing use of formal rules and procedures to regulate staff work processes. The most obvious symptom of increasing rule-orientation was the exponential increase in the colleges' consumption of paper, and in the proportion of documents giving instructions or procedural information.

As Gouldner (1954) points out, these processes serve to maintain control from the top and at the same time to increase the invisibility of power relations. In an institution traditionally characterized (despite a hierarchical structure) by relative openness of contact between levels, the operation of strict procedures governing contact between levels produced alienation, frustration, and a strong sense of powerlessness among rank-and-file staff.

The word 'bureaucracy' was rarely used explicitly in connection with these changes, but the word 'management' was. 'Management' as a descriptive term is, of course, relatively neutral: what is significant is not the introduction of the idea of attempting more efficiently to 'manage' an institution, but the particular form of management applied. Pre-eminently it was seen as a device for exerting control from the top. Essentially it was — in Burns and Stalker's terms (1966) — a 'mechanistic' rather than an 'organismic' concept of management owing more to the 'rational', 'scientific' models of industrial management than to traditionally applied models of academic decision-making. There was, as we have seen, a move to stricter role-differentiation, a growing rigidity in the hierarchy of command; information — using Burns' and Stalker's image — flowed upwards through filters while decisions and instructions were passed downwards through amplifiers. Critically, for the staff at the base of the structure, knowledge of the total picture was increasingly restricted to those at the top, leaving rank and file in a weakening position to question what was going on. The process of planning for CNAA validation greatly concentrated this restriction of knowledge (and power), for the CNAA, unlike the local university, was a geographically remote validating body, and knowledge of its requirements and expectations was not available through personal contact. Staff came to depend on designated intermediaries or 'gate-keepers' (Barnes, 1979) who passed down carefully selected pieces of information to meet immediate needs. The operation of this process in many CNAA-validated institutions is strongly confirmed in a study of validation undertaken by one of us (Alexander and Wormald, 1982): not only does the 'gatekeeper' device greatly enhance the power of those 'in the know' (and the consequent frustration and alienation of those in the dark) but the information itself can actively be changed in the process to meet the interests of those who convey it. 'What the CNAA requires' is in effect what a college intermediary chooses to say that the CNAA requires.

By contrast, 'organismic' management depends not on restricted-member knowledge but on the reverse — on each individual having a sense of the overall purpose and situation of the institution as a whole — so that there can be greater role flexibility to meet new needs. Roles are not fixed but are constantly redefined. Control is not concentrated at the top but is spread on a network basis. Communication is omni-directional rather than merely vertical, and includes information and advice rather than merely decisions and instructions. Where mechanistic management emphasizes obedience and loyalty to hierarchic superiors, organismic management emphasizes loyalty to the task in hand. Where the former expects members' sights to be fixed exclusively on the fulfilment of their defined responsibilities, the latter encourages broader perspectives and affiliations. Where, in the former, categories are clear and fixed, in the latter they are blurred and changeable.

The most fundamental criticism of mechanistic management is that it is premised on stability and is thereby unsuited to conditions of rapid change. By contrast, organismic management is adapted to unstable conditions. Yet, paradoxically, the essentially mechanistic/bureaucratic styles of management were introduced as seeming to offer the best possible way of enabling the colleges to cope with changes on a scale not previously experienced, as offering a guarantee of 'efficiency' in place of mere 'muddling through'.

A very different criticism concerns the applicability of this approach in academic communities. For the bureaucratic/mechanistic emphasis on strict role differentiation, unquestioning loyalty backed by sanctions, and limited task-orientation, is in strong opposition to the traditional academic/professional ethic of role-diffuseness, commitment to principles of inquiry and discovery, freedom of thought and action. It seeks and depends on a consensus which is quite strongly out of tune with the espoused pluralist ideology of academics in Britain (Bailey, 1977). By reducing the teacher's role to that of mere 'operative' or 'employee', it threatens the very basis of his traditional claim to professionalism.

Now, no model is an exact reflection of a particular practical condition: rather, such models indicate extremes and tendencies.

However, it seems to us that they have clear applicability in institutions of the sort we are concerned with. Lortie (1973) compares a 'managerial' and a 'devolved' power model which are very similar to Burns and Stalker's mechanistic/organismic polarity. He also suggests that the latter is the university model. This, we suspect, is fanciful: it is true that in Britain universities are less obviously centralized than polytechnics and colleges of higher education, and certainly that they make rather less overt use of the vocabulary of industrial management. Their departments undoubtedly have greater autonomy than do polytechnic departments and, of course, the ideology of personal autonomy is nowhere more strenuously upheld than in universities. But the very autonomy at the level which matters most — that of the department — is itself a guarantee of lack of uniformity. For university departments are institutions-within-institutions, and they can be run on very varying lines. Some are rigid and centralized, with a concentration of power at head-of-department level far stronger than could ever occur in a polytechnic. Departmental autonomy in universities can produce autocracy and mechanistic management or it can produce democracy and organismic management, while paradoxically the very inflexibility of mechanistic management procedures in some LEA-maintained institutions may themselves provide a degree of safeguard for the individual against the abuse of power at this level by stipulating strict rules of decision-making procedure (which of course will always be bent or circumvented by some). In some cases, then, the difference may be at the level of rhetoric only — centralization versus devolution, consensus versus pluralism, collectivism versus autonomy — rather than reality.

Yet we suggest that while it is difficult to locate decision-making in universities, at least at departmental level, these analytical categories do have relevance to the larger, maintained-sector institutions. What is more important is that mechanistic management is built into the CNAA's view of innovation and institutional decision-making: CNAA requirements make overt and substantial use of criteria like 'staff cohesiveness', 'mechanisms for course control' (with the emphasis on 'control' — see Alexander, 1979) and 'co-ordination'. There is a normative pull in the maintained sector towards centralization and bureaucratization to which the CNAA as the major validating body contributes significantly. It is notable that when universities validate colleges they give little attention to the institutional context and to decision-making — concentrating mainly on course content and staff competence. For the CNAA, the 'adequacy' of the institution is all-important and recent cases (Teesside, Huddersfield, Glasgow) show how potent can be their finding institutions 'inadequate' in this regard.

The history of the CNAA explains this emphasis — which, it might be thought, could well seem inconsistent with the sort of values one might expect to find in a major academic body which espouses academic democracy. The CNAA was formed from the old National Council for Technical Awards which validated technical/vocational courses in colleges of advanced technology and technical colleges (see Lane, 1975; Davis, 1980). The CNAA's membership and modes of conduct during its formative years were dominated by concepts and styles of organization and innovation imported from industry. This tradition persists not only in the official expectations about college decision-making, but also, as we shall see in the next section, in the assumptions about course planning and course structure.

Now, colleges like Enlands and Charlesford evolved from a different tradition, and it is notable that the Weaver reforms owed more to the university model of decision-making than to that evolving elsewhere in the LEA sector. These institutions, in transferring to CNAA validation, rapidly adopted styles of management which were totally unfamiliar and indeed out of tune with the dominant 'literary-romantic' college of education ethos (Taylor, 1969). The subsequent problems were a result both of this unfamiliarity and of the speed of change. The institutions were naïve and inexperienced in such matters, and the changes were sometimes enforced by individuals having all the zeal of converts. By contrast, polytechnic management styles, while firmly rooted in the mechanistic tradition, have evolved and adapted with the growth of the institutions. The institution 'going CNAA' may have to change overnight and its style of management may be crudely imitative while the polytechnics could adapt their versions of centralized management to particular circumstances. Moreover, while this style emphasizes the importance of specialist 'technical' knowledge, the one area of knowledge usually conspicuously absent in colleges of education/higher education was management knowledge (i.e. as an area of academic study). By contrast, many polytechnics offer management courses and have close and reciprocal links with industry. They have available, if they wish to use them, expertise in management rooted both in academic theorizing and industrial experience and are in a position to take a more relaxed, more flexible and realistic view of the process.

The consequences of rigid decision-making structures were thus accentuated by the speed of change — individual alienation, the evolution of alternative strategies to enable groups and individuals to by-pass middle hierarchic levels, the setting-up of yet more committees and what Burns and Stalker call the 'mechanistic jungle' (1966) — the setting up of specialist units to deal with problems which themselves depended for their survival on the perpetration of these problems. Thus, typically, staff development or course development might be seen as 'problems' unable to be resolved by existing procedures, so staff development and course development units would be set up whose officers would then tend to work to ensure that the 'problematic' perception, or at least the need for their work, remained in order to maintain their positions (especially when in the mid-1970s (as again at present) institutions were having to think seriously about compulsory redeployment and redundancy): quangoism and self-perpetuating oligarchies are features of educational institutions as well as of government.

Attendant upon and consistent with this shift in decision-making style in the colleges was a view of course development which likewise owed something to the (perceived or real) expectations of the validating body to which both colleges had changed. One of us (Alexander, 1979) has explored the 'CNAA model' in some detail and we do not propose to repeat in full the analysis. Briefly, the argument is as follows: while the CNAA can (and does) reasonably claim to judge individual course proposals on their merits, it imposes a general view of what constitutes a course which is applied to all proposals and which sets substantial constraints on colleges' freedom to plan as they wish. Moreover, the CNAA operates a particular model of curriculum development which has important consequences for courses in action. Essentially, this model is a means–end production-line one: planning → validation → implementation → evaluation. The focal point for validation is thus not what teachers and students actually do but what course planners *say* they will do. It is a *plan* which is validated, not an activity; a paper course rather than a course in action. This enforced disjunction between planning and action gives the prespecified plan considerable force, as blueprint or law, and the course committee (a management requirement of the CNAA) considerable power as enforcer of this 'law'. The emphasis is upon predictability and closure, and the central validation criterion is 'will it work?': course structure, course logistics and course control predominate. Thus in this model the individual teacher is an operative on the curriculum production line and evaluation become a process of testing the extent to which consistency has been achieved between plan and action.

This approach is contrasted with a view of curriculum development as continuous rather than once and for all, of a concept of curriculum in which action is pre-eminent, in which curriculum can never be wholly predictable since it is made and re-made by the encounters of particular students, staff, materials and ideas in unique, unrepeatable circumstances. By this view the 'plan' is something to be interpreted rather than 'implemented'. The gap between plan and action is recognized as necessary and inevitable, reflecting (a) the time-lag involved, (b) the perennial gulf between words and deeds, and (c) the gap between statements made for public (i.e. CNAA) consumption and private intentions — the rhetoric/reality gap. The emphasis shifts from intentions and outcomes to *means*, from structure and logistics to rationale and pedagogy, from the criterion 'will it work?' to 'is it educationally sound?' Above all, innovation is seen not as a single terminal process but as a continuous and cumulative one, in which the most that can be accorded any written plan or stated intentions is that they represent a hypothesis to be tested and probably modified.

For many teachers the mechanistic concept of curriculum provided a culture shock stronger even than mechanistic styles of management, for it constituted a threat much more profound: one which involved their professional self-image at its deepest level. For those who saw teaching as open, idiosyncratic, creative, always a unique blend of personal style and particular occasion, the introduction of a fairly crude scientism could be deeply disturbing. More than that, it constituted an assault on individual academic autonomy far more substantial than what many colleges thought they were escaping from by transferring from university to CNAA validation: *institutional* autonomy was enhanced, but not that of the individual, who saw control of his professional action and even to some extent of his professional thinking, transferred to course-management bodies in the interests of speed, efficiency and economy, and in the name of democracy, collectivism and participation.

Before returning to evaluation, to consider how it fits into this background of changed concepts and practices of college management and course design, let us remind ourselves of three earlier-stated premisses. Firstly, that many of the difficulties experienced by the institutions we have described stem from incongruences or inconsistencies within and between the various central elements in academic decision-making — college management, course management, innovation processes and evaluation procedures. Secondly, that further difficulties stem from inconsistencies within each of these between what is claimed for them and how they actually operate — their 'rhetoric' and their 'reality'. Thirdly, that the way forward to educational and institutional development having the support of the majority of staff and the best chance of success is to remove these inconsistencies where possible.

The major areas of such inconsistency were, in the present case, as follows:

1 Between the vision and claim of 'democracy' and the suppression of dissent in practice.

2 Between the espoused emphasis on pluralism and the normative pressure towards consensus.

3 Between the espoused goal of maximum participation and the reality of minority rule.

4 Between the post-Weaver college-of-education tradition of collective decision-making and the imported mainstream maintained-sector tradition of mechanistic management.

5 Between the tradition of individual academic autonomy and the pressure to achieve uniformity and display collective commitment and cohesiveness.

6 Between a view of curriculum innovation as a gradual, evolutionary process of hypothesis-testing and that of the curriculum as something to be planned in detail, then implemented in strict accordance within the plan.

7 Between the rhetoric of 'grass-roots' planning and the reality of centralization.

8 Between the assumption of an empirical-rational strategy and the reality of a power-coercive one.

9 Between a view of educational decisions as rooted in deeper, open and value-laden questions of educational desirability, and a view of such decision-making as essentially concerned with utility and feasibility.

6

THE INTEGRITY OF EVALUATION

The challenge of the integrity criterion

Despite the general inadequacies of the processes of decision-making and management we have described, and despite the inconsistencies which they demonstrate, they do — after a fashion — work, at least in respect of some people and some decisions. For while the processes seem not wholly consistent with those political and intellectual ideals which one might assume would be combined nowhere if not in a west European higher-education institution — democracy, value-pluralism, academic autonomy, the pursuit of truth — they are in fact the norm, rather than the exception, and tend to be reinforced in the maintained sector of higher education by key interests like local authorities and the CNAA. In terms of the external forms in the educational ritual they produce results: courses are planned, validated and implemented; students are recruited, taught, examined and awarded degrees. In terms of the underlying curricular and educational meanings of these rituals one might be considerably less convinced, for this would be to invoke a set of criteria for judging the worth of educational ventures which might be somewhat at variance with those of expediency and instrumentality.

But in a book on evaluation we cannot avoid these alternative criteria, for evaluation is about valuing, and educational evaluation is doubly value-laden. If it is to have any use other than as a purely cosmetic device for satisfying the demands of a validating body, or for servicing the power requirements of institutional oligarchies, evaluation has to be accepted as challenging, uncomfortable, untidy and potentially disturbing to an institution's equilibrium. For evaluation must exist, at least in part, to expose and clarify value issues — the varieties of educational goals and priorities for educational programmes, and the varieties of criteria for judging the quality and effectiveness of these programmes (see House, 1973).

This being so, evaluation must be seen both as problematic in its own terms and problematic for the context of management and decision-making in which it is set. For ultimately, it seems to us, while an evaluation must be useful and should provide practical support to teachers, course planners and administrators, it must meet a further criterion, that of *integrity*. The kernel of the evaluation 'problem' is a basic concern with knowledge and truth, and the 'integrity' criterion is, simply, an imperative which in an academic institutional context an evaluator can no more ignore than can the historian or scientist. The problem for institutional evaluation is that the integrity criterion has somehow to be upheld in the face of strong contrary pressures and constraints — time, limited resources, organizational problems, for example, but above all the risk of evaluation's use, abuse or neutralization to further or protect individual or sectional interests. (A tension perceptively explored, in relation to project evaluation, by MacDonald, 1981.)

We now need to explore the particular meanings of 'integrity' which we apply to the practice of evaluation, and the particular ways in which these meanings might come into conflict with the institutional processes we have so far discussed.

The inevitability of pluralism

We have identified what we perceive as a gap between the espoused democratic/participatory ideology of institutions like Enlands and Charlesford and their bureaucratic/mechanistic decision-making processes. To 'work', these processes had to assume, or create, consensus about goals and the means of achieving them.

This is a fairly basic tension in organized life, of course — between the commitment to widespread participation in the decision-making process and the need actually to make decisions. An educational institution has a strong instrumental function and if it fails to fulfil this function efficiently, quickly and cheaply the consequences can be serious. In Enlands and Charlesford in the mid-to-late 1970s, as in most higher-education institutions at the present time, the overriding imperative was to create courses which would recruit sufficient students to keep staff fully employed. In this climate the all-talk-no-action circularity of 'democratic' discussion of policy issues would tend to be dismissed with impatience and frustration, and it was probably inevitable that — whether consciously or unconsciously — the model for educational management, for 'making things happen', was the industrial production-line, input/output approach discussed above (see pp. 151–60).

However, we are not convinced that this is either the only management model available or the only one which works, and see as a critical challenge facing educational institutions the need to reconcile the two imperatives of participation and efficiency. For in such institutions mechanistic management is not merely inconsistent with claimed institutional values but so strongly so that it can be less rather than more efficient than more open, flexible and participatory forms in that it produces conflict and alienation. Consensus can be dissembled (as it frequently is for CNAA validation) and can even be 'demonstrated' through voting procedures, but it can never be enforced at the level which matters most — that of the individual teacher, on whose conviction about what he does the quality of a student's education partly depends.

A college introducing an institutional evaluation can choose whether to make the evaluation consistent with the claimed ideology or with the organizational reality. If the latter path is chosen, the evaluation will be non-problematic because it will simply be an extension of existing management practices and will exist to serve and support those practices. If the former path is chosen, and attempts are made to make the evaluation programme organizationally consistent with democratic/participatory ideology, problems may ensue. This was the dilemma at both colleges. At Charlesford the evaluation constitution, as we have seen, was 'democratic' and pluralist, so that by exposing alternative viewpoints and judgements and by exploring issues deemed as important by competing interests it served to threaten the security or at least equanimity of course management bodies. At Enlands the evaluation ran into the same problem but in a different way: here there was a contradiction between the commitment to institutional self-study and the means by which the project was to be controlled. The problem was exacerbated by the evaluator's concern for the project's 'integrity' in relation to the self-study brief. In both cases some studies could be accommodated despite the mismatch between evaluation aspirations and management realities — those that reported 'facts' which were bland, non-controversial and non-threatening, which were consistent with the prevailing orthodoxy. Studies which offered glimpses of alternative viewpoints, particularly if these diverged substantially from orthodox perceptions, were very difficult to accommodate.

Somehow, this matter has to be resolved, *for there is little doubt that plurality is a fact of institutional life* to which the integrity condition for evaluation demands attention. It is not merely a plurality of values, such as is inherent in all educational ventures: what is a 'good' course, an 'effective' lecturer, a 'successful' student; what is the best way to train teachers; what sort of qualities does a good teacher need; how should a teacher-training course relate to educational change — by producing a teacher who conforms to and perpetuates established norms and practices or one who works to change them? And so on. The plurality goes beyond such matters of opinion, it includes 'fact' as well as value: it concerns the basic status of the information on which decisions are made. Formal evaluation has been defined (Cronbach, 1963; Stufflebeam, 1971) as the 'provision of information for decision-makers' and the essence of its justification as a distinct activity is that such 'information', systematically gathered and presented, is inherently more 'reliable' than hunch or belief, and the decisions made are therefore more likely to be right, or at least can be defended (tautologously perhaps) as 'informed'.

Fact or value? A note on evaluation methodology

What then is the status of information presented as a result of formal evaluation processes? What claims can legitimately be made for data gathered by means of techniques available to evaluators which cannot be made with such assurance about judgements rooted in experience and common sense? The answers involve a discussion of methodology more detailed than we can offer in a book concerned mainly with the institutional context of evaluation, and in any case there are available numerous excellent discussions of methodology *per se* (e.g. Anderson, *et. al.*, 1975; Tyler *et al.*, 1967; Popham *et al.*, 1969; Hamilton *et al.*, 1977, etc.) But institutional practices in relation to management and innovation have a critical connection with ideas about what constitutes valid evaluation and about what sort of evaluation evidence can be relied upon, to which we must devote some attention.

One of the difficulties here is the extent to which the methodological scene is depicted in terms of polarities: the 'illuminative' method of Parlett and Hamilton (1972), or the 'responsive' procedures of Stake (1976), or the 'curriculum criticism' of Mann (1978) and Eisner (1979), on the one hand, are presented as standing in a mutually exclusive relationship to the objectives-referenced methodologies of, say, Tyler (1971) or Gagné (1972) or Bloom *et al.* (1971).

The protagonists themselves in this debate have usually been careful to identify the extent of shared territory and the polarities are as often as not set up by writers of textbooks or teachers of evaluation concerned to restructure the arguments in terms amenable to the outsider. Moreover, while a 'research community' can achieve, on the basis of its members' depth of engagement with the issues as specialists, a reasonable sophistication in methodological discussion, this is less likely where institutional evaluation is concerned. Here, the 'community' comprises the institution's inhabitants, very few of whom, if any, will have made evaluation methods their central academic or professional interest; they are, after all, contracted as staff or admitted as students to devote their time to other areas of concern, challenging enough in themselves. Consequently, institutional discourse about evaluation is conducted very much at the common-sense level, with communication facilitated by the ready use of dichotomies. Here are three on which we can comment briefly:

1 'Pure' research is contrasted with 'impure' evaluation. Institutional evaluation cannot be controlled or experimental, and judged by mainstream research standards it may appear to be 'contaminated', *ex post facto* and methodologically imperfect. It takes place in working educational settings, is subject to practical and political constraints and is usually conducted by non-specialists. Clearly the legitimacy of conclusions from an evaluation study needs to be demonstrated, but criteria for legitimation applied to social science research are not necessarily the most apposite for institutional evaluation studies. Methodology as such is perhaps less significant here than what is claimed for and done with the 'findings'. If factual accuracy is claimed, then it is right to scrutinize an evaluation study's methods and conclusions in these terms, checking on sampling, statistical treatment and so on; not a few evaluation studies would fail this test. However, as some of our examples showed, the role of an evaluation conducted as a part of an institution's continuing processes of debate and development indicates that other criteria can be invoked.

2 A study is either 'objective' or 'subjective'. In everyday discourse 'objective' and 'subjective' usually appear as mutually exclusive categories, incorporating the assumptions that objectivity is an

absolute, that it is achievable and that it is a higher plane of thinking and being than 'mere' subjectivity. Without entering what we recognize to be an intellectual minefield, we would suggest that at least an awareness that it is a minefield needs to pervade institutional discussion on such matters. For example, do not 'subjective' values and perspectives inform 'objective' as well as interpretative methods; how else do we decide on which test items to include or omit, what words to put in our semantic scale? Perhaps the methods of analysis are more 'objective' in that they have been publicly devised and corroborated, and are therefore open to external scrutiny, but what goes into the original evaluation instrument may well be as rooted in 'subjective' views of knowledge, learning, development and behaviour as what goes into an interview schedule; 'Under the rug of technique lies an image of man' (Eisner, 1969).

3 Studies are 'scientific' or 'unscientific'. By this judgement the methodology of the physical sciences is seen as providing the only legitimate route to the truth, and other approaches are judged not in terms of their distinctive claims but in terms of their failure to be 'science'. The judgement perhaps reflects a view of science as the rational pursuit of indisputable facts and immutable laws about the 'real' world, which contrasts with the vagaries of intuition and common sense on the one hand, and on the other with artistic endeavour as the construction of internal, private worlds which cannot be publicly demonstrated to correspond with the real world 'outside'. Again, the scope for disputing the assumptions here is extensive; those concerning the nature of reality, for instance, have kept philosophers in business for centuries. Or again, scientists as well as artists might wish to dispute the implied view of their activities; both groups might wish to argue that in different ways each seeks truth and in pursuit of it offers statements which are open to verification, falsification or some form of external critical judgement; that each uses personal intuition and imagination as well as the publicly-accepted procedures, theories and forms; that creativity and rationality enter both scientific and artistic judgements and acts. Some would question the assumption that scientific knowledge, unlike artistic expression, produces final, unchangeable 'truths', and would point to the way that many apparently convincing scientific theories are eventually disproved or substantially modified:

Those among our theories which turn out to be highly resistant to criticism, and which appear to us at a certain moment in time to be better approximations to truth than other known theories, may be described, together with the reports of their tests, as the 'science' of that time. Since none of them can be positively justified, it is essentially their critical and progressive character — the fact that we can argue about their claim to solve our problems better than their competitors — which constitutes the rationality of science. (Popper, 1972, p. vii)

Others — not least physical scientists — might be sceptical of the claims of the human sciences, from which evaluation draws most of its methodology, to constitute a science at all, at least in terms of the vocabulary of laws, proof, causality, and so on. The grounds for this objection might be not only the methodology of the human sciences but the complexity of human behaviour. At this point they might be more inclined to commend the artist's concern to expose and explore the subtlety, diversity, richness but essential elusiveness of the human condition than the social scientist's attempts to superimpose on it categories and models; the artist's concern to portray rather than the social scientist's urge to explain: 'The soul wanted what it wanted. It had its own natural knowledge. It sat unhappily on superstructures of explanation, poor bird, not knowing which way to fly' (Bellow, 1971, p. 5).

Thus, beneath the pre-packaging of everyday discourse about evaluation methods, are issues which in exploration become more, rather than less, complex. But because evaluation is a practical activity the issue seen as most pressing is not so much 'which methods have the soundest theoretical basis in terms of their claims to produce a valid picture of events?' but 'which method will work best?' The contingent problems are those of resources, time, expertise and acceptability. A simple feedback questionnaire with a small number of closed responses is much more convenient than, say, a test or scale requiring computerized analysis, or open interviews which need to be transcribed from audio tapes (in itself a lengthy and tedious process) before analysis can begin. Some methods require a financial and human investment which is just not available in many institutions. A crucial difference between research-oriented evaluation, as in the funded project at Enlands, and institutional course evaluation, as at Charlesford, is that the latter has to be done quickly in order to be fed into decision-making while the course component is still warm: time is a major factor. Then there is the matter of acceptability: staff and students are most likely to participate in an evaluation (a) which makes minimal demands on their time, and (b) which will not expose their individual weaknesses to public scrutiny. The catalogue of such practical considerations is endless, and a number of them are discussed in this book.

Is it sufficient to take a thoroughly pragmatic view of evaluation methodology as is implied above? If we do so, evaluation becomes a more marketable commodity, to teachers and administrators alike. Some might argue, for example, that the debate about scientific method has little application to the murky and methodologically questionable field of evaluation. They might argue further that the invocation of such matters, however one views scientific method, weakens the claim of practical evaluation in two respects: firstly, because most evaluation fails to meet the observational and experimental criteria of the inductive method; secondly, because the Popperian position (page 167) produces a relativism which provides a respectable justification for those who oppose all evaluation but the private and self-referenced in that apparently it makes the *ad hoc* intuitive 'theory' as sustainable, in the absence of convincing evidence to the contrary, as that achieved more systematically.

However, the pragmatist's position is as open to abuse in institutionally-contextualized evaluation as the relativist's; the fact that such evaluation is generally decision/policy directed makes the status of the information it provides of some significance for those affected. Either way, then, methodology matters.

At the root of the debate is the fundamental question: 'What is the basis of our claim to know?' with the related questions concerning the nature of 'truth' and how we may approach it, of the nature and validity of empirical enquiry, 'proof' and 'evidence' and the provability of causal relationships.

If one accepts that an evaluation combines a purportedly accurate *description* of an educational circumstance with a *judgement* of its worth, one has to consider the status of descriptions and judgements in general. A description is a linguistic or otherwise symbolic representation of the external world and there are, to say the least, competing views about the point (if there is one) at which language and the external world might coincide. And a judgement of worth is ultimately an expression of personal value, an ethical statement rooted in individual beliefs and experiences, and as such cannot claim to be true or false. So educational evaluations are value-judgements based on what are debatable pictures of a 'real' world of courses, teaching and learning, and evaluators may need to accept that there can be no 'objectivity', only various degrees of subjectivity, and that the nearest they can get to an 'accurate' observation is to have private observations publicly tested and corroborated so that there is a measure of agreement that we have all seen the same thing, more or less. (C.F. Habermas, 1970: 'Objectivity is the consensus of subjectivities.')

If one's view of evaluation is of a process of feedback at the individual teacher level, if all one wants to undertake is a purely private activity, then objectification remains an academic issue, and one's judgements, or value judgements do not have to be justified. But once evaluation becomes the concern of more than one teacher, once it is used to inform policy decisions which will affect students, teachers and courses at the institutional level, we have an obligation to ensure that such evaluation is as well-founded, conceptually, as possible. And if, once one explores its epistemological basis, all evaluation can be shown to be of intrinsically limited reliability, certain policy implications seem to follow concerning how we should evaluate, how we should use evaluation findings, and how the process should be controlled.

Firstly, an evaluation programme methodology derived from a single discipline will compound its limitations and potential distortions. There is relative security to be gained from a stance of considered eclecticism deliberately drawing on contrasting methodologies.

Secondly, it would seem essential, particularly where decision-making is to be based on evaluation 'findings', to 'cover' one method by another — to use alterntive ways of representing and interpreting the educational encounter(s) in question with a view to juxtaposing them and exploring the extent of match or mismatch (c.f. the 'triangulation' principle developed in the Ford Teaching Project (Adelman, 1981a; Elliott, 1976).

Thirdly, it is important to recognize that while, methodologically, different perspectives or 'definitions of the situation' gained through 'triangulation' might seem equally valid, in practical institutional terms such definitions are more likely to be in competition. Moreover, the competition is an unequal one, and certain definitions may well be seen to 'matter' more than others — the teacher's more than the student's perhaps, or the administrator's more than the teacher's. The extent to which a plurality of views is permitted to be significant in evaluation is a function of the power structure of the institution. In this case the evaluator may feel that to preserve methodological integrity he has to redress the balance, to over-represent some views, to act perhaps, in Elliott's words, as 'underdog's advocate' (Elliott, 1977).

Fourthly, given what can be shown to be the rather shaky status of the 'objective fact' in evaluation methods, we might feel more favourably disposed towards overt subjectivity, more prepared to value the intuitive judgements of ourselves and others as much as the 'scientific' findings of evaluators, more inclined to see such intuitive judgements as evaluation data of potentially comparable validity to the findings of formal evaluation studies. Equally, it might be argued that we should be very cautious in the way we make decisions on the basis of evaluation 'findings': does the data really justify the decision?

Finally, if we are prepared to evaluate then perhaps we should also be prepared to submit our evaluation practices to the same critical scrutiny as our courses receive.

These conditions are required to maintain the integrity of institutional evaluation methods, caught as they are between the unattainable perfectionism of those who advocate an all-or-nothing research 'purity' and those who argue that precisely because this is unattainable, anything goes as long as it produces usable information. We believe there to exist a legitimate middle ground for the methodology of institutional evaluation, and hope that the Charlesford and Enlands evaluations exemplify it. (For other examples see, for example, Biott, 1979; Walkley, 1979; Powell *et al.*, 1980; Pienkowski and Cameron-Jones, 1980; Bioletti 1981; O'Neil, 1981; Wicksteed, 1981).

A clash of epistemologies

It will be perceived that this view of evaluation methodology contrasts markedly with the view required by the production-line model of curriculum development outlined earlier which we saw to be implicit in much current practice in the maintained sector of higher education, possibly reinforced by CNAA requirements. It will also be recognized that if evaluation knowledge is regarded as provisional and tentative, this has important implications for policy-making generally, not just for those areas of policy evolved from systematic evaluation studies. For all decisions rest on evaluations of some sort, on situational appraisals, on attempts to base decisions about what ought to happen on the best possible information about what is happening or what is likely to happen. *If the status of 'facts' gained from systematic evaluations using established methods can be shown to be in a fundamental sense questionable, how much more so may be the sorts of information on which most day-to-day institutional decision-making rests?* By this view policies can most usefully be regarded as hypotheses, theories or predictions.

Policy formulation and institutional decision-making ought to be subject to an approach analogous to scientific inquiry, namely, one of constant critical examination using the experience of implementing policy as a means not of proving, whatever the cost, that the policy was right but as a means of testing its validity, strengths and weaknesses. Similarly, a course submission to a validating body is not a master-plan to be 'implemented' but a hypothesis, the best available perhaps, which restates a particular problem (e.g. that of training teachers) and offers as a solution, a practical *theory* of instruction to be tried out, modified, used to refine the analysis of the problem itself as well as the solution, and so on.

However, the parallel between scientific inquiry and policy formulation/implementation can be pursued only up to a point, as Lubasz (1981) has pointed out. The trial-and-error approach requires some degree of consensus over standards, techniques and criteria for judgement among the community concerned; while in an educational institution this is achievable in procedural and organizational matters, it is more difficult where questions of curriculum purpose and content are concerned since these are inherently questions of value. Moreover, in a bounded, hierarchical educational institution, values are as likely to be positional as educational and the criteria for judging recommendations, decisions and policies will reflect individual and group views of what is fair and just.

Our analysis suggests a likelihood of conflict between the prevailing 'epistemology of management', with its emphasis on consensus, finality, proof, stability and efficiency, and our 'epistemology of educational evaluation' with its emphasis on value-pluralism, hypothesizing, change and the improvability of educational thought and practice. This is likely to be most acute in those institutions which adopt a more strongly scientistic, mechanistic approach to management, or an authoritarian one, and which underscore this by compartmentalizing the related functions of educational management, innovation, development and evaluation. The conflict will be less in institutions prepared to blur the organizational and conceptual boundaries and which allow elements of the 'epistemology of evaluation' to inform styles and processes of management.

Accountability, evaluation and the management of innovation: match and mismatch

The character and force of management and evaluation epistemologies within educational institutions, and the degree of congruence or conflict between them, is not simply a matter of style but a matter of human consequence. It was suggested earlier that the extent to which an evaluation agent or agency acknowledged institutional pluralism had consequences for the sort of methodology that might be used. Similarly there is an inter-dependent relationship between the strategies used to bring about innovation and the approach to evaluation, and between each of these and the prevailing accountability relations within an institution.

Although we are aware of the limitations of conceptualizing by means of ideal types, we think it is worthwhile using such means to complement our earlier exploration of relationships between innovation strategies, evaluation and the continuity of accountability relations maintained by management.

Management involves the everyday decisions which regulate actions and information within an institution with the intention of maintaining continuity and stability. Essentially management maintains the nature of the accountability relationships within the institution. Attempts at innovation may lead to change, to adjustment or to neither, but whatever its consequences, attempts at innovation introduce instability in some parts of the institution's systems. To regulate the introduction of innovation, the institution devises more or less complex and visible strategies for staging, delivering and monitoring the progress of the innovation. Evaluation — judging the worth and effectiveness of the innovation and its consequences — may be contemporaneous or it may follow on later after attempts at implementing the innovation. The range of evaluation approaches that may be adopted is directly dependent upon the accountability relationships and the strategies for innovation that the institution prefers and practices.

The relationships between management, strategies for innovation and evaluation are complex. One could discuss them simplistically in terms of match and mismatch between the three activities but as soon as one begins to give reasons for the match and mismatch, the complexities of these interrelationships are revealed. These three institutional activities have different histories of development reflected in the differences in the literature that is cited in each case. The body of knowledge, including that derived from research, that may be utilized by management, has been developing for at least eighty years, whereas the knowledge about and the very idea of 'strategies of innovation' are more recent (see Lewin, 1948; Weiner, 1968; Bennis, *et al.* 1976; Schon, 1971; Burns and Stalker, 1966). Evaluation, in the sense that it is used in this book, is an even more recent field of study than management and innovation, only emerging with any coherence in the 1960s. The ideas and practices of evaluation and the development of strategies of innovation are poorly understood compared to those relating to management, and one of the intentions of this book has been to enhance understanding of these three institutional activities and to foster discussion about their interrelationships. In times of stability or minor adjustment, the rhetoric/reality discrepancy in management practices may be unimpressive. However, when an institution wishes or is forced by external circumstances to bring about change internally, then the reality of the accountability relationships is displayed in the strategies employed to conduct the course of the innovation.

Trying to manage innovation has built-in contradictions. Management thrives on stability and predictability; innovation introduces uncertainty, it de-skills, and it produces relative instability. Strategies of managing innovation to bring about the desired changes can be planned and seen through with minimum deleterious consequences for human freedom and dignity. Unfortunately, perhaps partly due to ignorance of the interrelationship between these three activities, the strategies and their means of delivery are more often destructive of freedoms and lead to some degree of degradation of institutional life. There seem to be remarkably few managers in higher education with the imagination and verve that are required to develop and implement strategies of innovation whilst preserving human freedoms and dignity.

Ideal types

1 *Accountability*

In chapter 1 we set out and five 'ideal types' of accountability relationship within educational institutions (adapted from Alexander, 1980b). These were:

1 Managerial
2 Consultative
3 Mutual culpability
4 Professional autonomy
5 Proletarian

It will be seen that both Charlesford and Enlands illustrate a 'consultative'/'managerial' mixture, with the stricter 'managerial' relationship asserting itself at points where evaluation produced threatening data. It will also be seen that the more straightforward 'managerial' tradition of the polytechnic world into which, by virtue of their new affiliation with CNAA, both institutions moved, contrasted markedly with the culture of collegiality (Wyatt, 1977) of the former colleges of education, though we must emphasize that mutuality was only one element in that culture, a commitment or aspiration held by significant groups within the institutions, but sometimes at variance with the 'consultative' relations represented by the formal decision-making arrangements. Universities, we have suggested, are really institutions-within-institutions, or semi-autonomous states within a federal structure. That federal structure is bureaucratic and managerial/consultative, but at the department level one can find examples of all types of accountability relationship (Moodie and Eustace, 1974). Generally, at this level the 'professional autonomy' ethic is very powerful, and there is little evidence of collective action or mutual culpability, though there may be a semblance of mutuality in the *form* of departmental academic decision-making, or alternatively a sometimes rather toothless managerialism. In most cases, however, the individual's professional autonomy will be assumed. It is interesting in this context to compare the parallel ambience of the unions concerned. The university teachers' union, AUT, upholds individual autonomy and has had some difficulty in mobilizing members to act collectively over matters like salaries at times when, as until very recently, their autonomy and security remained unthreatened: for many, the latter were more precious than salary comparabilities across the binary line. The now defunct college of education union, ATCDE, had a pronounced collegiality, verging on the genteel, and redolent even into the late sixties of Miss Beale and Miss Buss; this contrasted starkly with the polytechnic/further education union, ATTI, with which ATCDE merged during the 1970s reorganization and cutback of teacher education to form the present NATFHE. In ATTI, as now in the enlarged NATFHE, the battle-lines between employer and employee were clear and unbridgeable, and of the three former unions it most resembled its industrial counterparts. Undoubtedly there was congruence between management, accountability climate and union ethos in each case, though the direction of the influence is hard to establish.

The accountability relationships that are considered in what will follow are those that we term 'managerial', 'consultative' and 'mutual culpability'. These have already been described in detail in chapter 1. The other two ideal types, 'professional autonomy' and 'proletarian', are not considered in relation to innovation strategies and evaluation. 'Professional autonomy' in an extreme form is manifest when academics declare themselves and the discipline they represent as sacrosanct, accountable only to themselves and their own criteria of worth. In its extreme form, 'professional autonomy' has no common ground at all with institutional self-evaluation, which of course is premissed on *collective* endeavour, relationships and responsibility. 'Proletarian' accountability relationships have been described as part of the life, for instance, of the Chinese communes and within such western institutions as the free universities of Berlin and London, which emerged in the late 1960s. At its roots, 'proletarian' accountability considers that the student has the capability and responsibility to define and negotiate what is to be the content and form of his curriculum. This form of institutional epistemology requires considerable or even absolute consensus over the aims and values underpinning institutional practices, and over the educational worth of these practices. 'Proletarian' accountability produces a form of public self-criticism of the worth of one's activities in relation to these ideals. This is so unusual in the West and most other parts of the world, that we have no direct experience of such practices. In our experience the practices most resembling the 'proletarian' type, apart from the free universities already mentioned, were the school meetings held by

A.S. Neill at Summerhill and the 'Moot' held at Countesthorpe College in the 1970s (Bernbaum, 1975).

2 Managing innovation

We take our three types of management of innovation strategies from Bennis *et al.* (1976). In our thinking about the institutions with which we were involved as evaluation agents and in our studies of other institutions, we find that the ideas of Bennis *et al.* seem best to fit analysis. The three terms for the types refer to strategies for effecting planned educational change. The strategies indicate procedures for the formulation and adoption of innovation. Implementation of these three approaches is through the maintenance of continuity of accountability relationships by management.

'Power-coercive' strategies rely on the political/administrative system for their effectiveness. They involve statutes, include legislation, political pressure groups and election, as well as using guilt and shame as legitimate means of furthering ends. Power-coercive strategies may be effective in the stages of formulation and adoption of innovation, but implementation which requires changes in norms, roles and relationships is difficult to achieve by this approach.

'Empirical-rational' strategies assume that man is reasonable and will act in some rational way. The knowledge presented during the formulation, adoption and implementation stages of the innovation would be seen by the adopters as 'objective', based upon research that is itself unbiased in terms of interest groups. However, the question of the redistribution of power in the system is not usually taken into account and the continuance of the current structure is taken for granted. It may be that systems adopt empirical-rational strategies especially at the innovation and perhaps adoption stages, when knowledge does not threaten members' status.

'Normative re-educative' strategies regard the question of how the client understands his problems as of central importance. The problem of innovation is not a matter of supplying the appropriate technical information but rather a matter of changing attitudes, skills, values and relationships. In the normative re-educative approach a change agent works with the client. The change agent seeks to avoid manipulation of the client by bringing the values of the client into the open and by working through value conflicts in a responsive manner. The change agent may concentrate on improving the problem-solving capabilities of a system by developing and fostering the institutional-isation of problem-solving strategies and processes (institutional self-study, perhaps leading to institutional self-evaluation). Another approach is to release and foster growth of awareness in persons within a system. This approach is based on the belief that persons are capable of creative action if conditions are made more favourable.

3 The conduct of evaluation

The set of principles and procedures for conducting the evaluation that the evaluation agent or agency may use are adapted from MacDo-nald (1976a). These are 'bureaucratic', 'democratic' and 'autonomous' (termed 'autocratic' by MacDonald).

The bureaucratic ('hired hand') evaluation matches the control in power-coercive institutions. The bureaucratic evaluation agent serves the needs of senior administration.

The democratic ('honest broker') evaluation meets the needs of normative re-educative institutions where access and response to information is available to all members.

The autonomous evaluation entails the use of evaluation 'experts' with esoteric knowledge of how to conduct 'objective' evaluations. The autonomous evaluation agent takes attempts by any staff to influence the procedures or content of the evaluation as introducing a form of 'contamination' to the design and thus, to an extent, as making the evaluation invalid. The criteria of validity to which the auton-omous agent or agency expresses allegiance aspire to be universalistic: the generalizable findings of research conducted via methodologies having some extent of claim to 'objective' or 'scientific' status. The relationship between these generalized findings and methodologies and the specific issues or problems of a particular institution do not become a basis for discussions about 'validity' or 'objectivity' with the evaluation agent.

As the agent or agency claims immunity, through context-free methodology and claims for the 'truth' and generalizability of research findings external to those of the specific cases in the institution, we term this type of evaluator 'autonomous'. Note, however, the strong reservations we have expressed about such claims in respect of evalua-tion earlier in this chapter, and how we come to define an evaluation's integrity (i.e. autonomy) in a way which places rather greater em-phasis on its acknowledgement of the plurality of goals, perspectives, perceptions of reality and truth in educational institutions, and the way these are position-related rather than random, and rather less emphasis on supposedly context-free truth or objectivity claims.

Matching

If there is consonance between accountability relationships, strategies of innovation and the principles and procedures used by evaluation agents or agencies, then the following typology emerges:

	Accountability context	Innovation strategy	Evaluation strategy
Type 1	Managerial	Power-coercive	Bureaucratic
Type 2	Consultative	Rationale empirical	Autonomous
Type 3	Mutual culpability	Normative/ re-educative	Democratic

What kinds of innovations are these institutional Types 1–3 capable of? We suggest that Type 1 institutions, for instance, could introduce new programmes and courses of study and would do so ensuring that organizational components like the academic department, the committee structure or the status and power of individuals would be maintained. Goals such as crossing the established boundaries of knowledge, regrouping staff, or rotating positions of power and authority tend not to be within the ambit of institutions of Type 1. Senior management would tend to prefer an evaluation agent or agency which could be trusted or required to raise topics and issues and choose modes of investigation in such a way as to maintain the status quo, i.e. bureaucratic evaluation.

Type 2 institutions collect information pertinent to their development needs. The information to be collected is predominantly that required by the senior managers on the basis of what they define as the future needs of the institution. Agendas emerging from the collection of such information may be discussed in committees or other bodies which other members of staff may attend. The committees which are elected through 'democratic' processes may engage in deliberations leading to some form of decision, eventually, but the top decision-making forum, perhaps chaired by the head of the institution, faculty, department or course, gives the concluding and final decision on earlier deliberations. We have already mentioned the role of the autonomous evaluator in Type 2 institutions.

We believe Type 1 and particularly Type 2 would encompass the majority of educational institutions.

Institutions of Type 3 are very unusual. Between us we know of few educational institutions which we consider could be placed as this type. In Type 3 institutions the overriding goal of accountability relationships and strategies of innovation is improving the quality of the educational experiences for both students *and staff* (on the assumption that learning is socially embedded and conditioned, and therefore the situation of staff and the quality of institutional life are powerful influences on, and thus matter as much as, the learning experiences of students). The introduction of innovation which brings about change and adjustment may mean that changes in occupational role, formal organizational structures and the epistemological bases of academic activities are necessary to the pursuit of ways of implementing innovation in ways most beneficial to the institution's activities. The rigid continuity of academic positions, structures, salary differentials and knowledge boundaries might need to be replaced by the establishment of relations which relate to developments arising from the evaluation.

Given the involvement of staff in the strategies of innovation and the mutual culpability acknowledged by the management, the form of evaluation in Type 3 would acknowledge the 'right to know' of all members of the institution and would be responsive to issues arising across the institution. The principles and procedures of the evaluation agenda would then be close to those expressed by MacDonald as 'democratic', and close to the ideals expressed in the Charlesford evaluation constitution.

This use of ideal types and our attempts at matching must be treated with caution. Models invariably over-simplify, they

> impose a seeming rationality and order, and a network of logical and reciprocal relationships, on areas of human activity frequently characterized by irrationality, disorder, illogic and *ad hoc*ery. . . . They tend to imply a static relationship between categories, aspects or elements where such relationships are in reality dynamic and constantly changing through time and space. (Alexander, 1980a)

We might add that it would be strange indeed in a discussion of evaluation in educational institutions which made so much of the complexity of institutional life, of plurality, of multiple perspectives and levels of meaning and explanation, of incongruence between word and deed, claim and action, and so on, if we ended by encapsulating all this complexity in three types of institution and three dimensions of institutional life (Wildavsky, 1979). The models are intended to be suggestive rather than conclusive, and in particular to serve to emphasize two central arguments of this present chapter. Firstly, that the integrity of the evaluation process (an elusive goal in itself) is, in institutional evaluation, critically dependent on aspects of institutional life which conventionally fall outside the boundaries of methodological discussion, management and innovation styles and procedures, and accountability assumptions and relations; and these aspects demand attention by those developing evaluation programmes and procedures. Secondly, that notwithstanding this institutional or contextual re-interpretation of the methodological 'problem' in evaluation, that problem, even as re-interpreted, remains at root a substantially epistemological one, since all decision-making (not merely formal evaluation) rests on claims to know.

7 TOWARDS THE SELF-EVALUATING INSTITUTION

In this book we have used practical experience as a basis for defining the central issues in institutional self-evaluation and for identifying a theoretical framework within which others might analyse their institutional situation in relation to the management of change generally and of evaluation in particular. We hope we have been honest and fair in our exploration of the problems and difficulties yet have also shown that an adequately-conceived and properly organized evaluation programme is feasible, and can make an important contribution to that collective 'theorizing' on which we believe the health, indeed the validity, of an educational institution to depend.

'Problems' in evaluation, avoidable or necessary?

It is as well to repeat our view of the status of the 'problems' we have discussed. We mentioned in the Introduction that we went into the practice of institutional self-evaluation armed with a certain amount of knowledge of existing evaluation theory and practice, but conscious of how little of this was applicable to what we and our institutions were attempting and therefore in different ways each of us was working in the dark. We encountered problems, sometimes trivial, sometimes severe. Our initial reaction was to seek explanations for these problems in terms of the 'inadequacy' either of the approach we were adopting or of the institution itself. Standing now well back from the experiences and placing them as we have done in a broader analytical framework, we can perceive two sets of problems. Firstly, those relating to the organizational frameworks for evaluation: matters like human and material resources, the acute pressure of time, the restrictions on methodology, the challenge of achieving adequate dissemination and discussion and so on. Many of the problems in this category are avoidable: we have tried to identify those which can be anticipated and resolved in the evaluation planning process, and have outlined earlier (pp. 23–4) the sorts of decisions which have to be taken in this regard.

The second category of problems emerged only once our evaluation programmes began to deliver findings which challenged existing values, orthodoxies and interests. We had, of course, anticipated that institutional self-evaluation posed difficulties of a political as well as a technical nature — this is clearly adumbrated in the Charlesford evaluation constitution and a defusing response to these is represented by the Charlesford evaluation mechanism. (We remain surprised at the extent to which the rapidly expanding interest in evaluation in schools and higher education seriously neglects the political dimension.) But we had perhaps underestimated how far our evaluations would challenge the institutions' assumptions and mechanisms *beyond* those of immediate concern to the evaluation programmes. Course evaluation, we had assumed, would pose most threat to, and produce most resistance from, course teachers, so that their security and confidence needed to be safeguarded. In practice, as we have shown, the challenge spread outwards from courses to encompass the organizational and ideological context in which the courses were embedded, the principles on which institutional decision-making claimed to rest, the processes of management, decision-making and innovation.

We now see the extensiveness of this challenge as an inevitable and wholly desirable consequence of evaluation. In fact we would now be somewhat suspicious of any claim that an evaluation whose processes and outcomes can be painlessly accommodated represents a serious attempt at evaluation at all. We would expect to be able to question its adequacy on a number of counts. How truly comprehensive was its focus? Did it grapple with basic value issues or merely concern itself with externals like admission and assessment statistics? To whom was it disseminated? Were all findings made widely available? Who controlled its focus and conduct? What sort of methods did it use — were they directed at producing findings which created an impression of consensus and neutrality or did they seek to identify different analyses of the 'facts'? Would all members of the institution's community accept the claim that evaluation had essentially confirmed the validity of the status quo? Had they been asked for their interpretation of the findings? Who had made the claim on behalf of them and the rest of the institution?

We would commend these questions, and others suggested in the previous chapters, to those now beginning to 'evaluate evaluations' on behalf of, for example, CNAA course and institutional review panels.

The alternative, it seems to us, is an increase in 'token evaluation' which might satisfy formalities, but at the expense of staff time, institutional resources, the credibility of evaluation generally, and the achievement of significant educational progress.

Levels of evaluation

We identified in chapter 1 three main types of evaluation in current use — student/pupil performance assessment, intention appraisal as undertaken by validating bodies, and the expanding field of course/ curriculum evaluation which can encompass educational intentions, processes and outcomes. Subsequently we subdivided the latter into individual or private self-appraisal undertaken with a view to achieving efficiency, productivity and, perhaps, improvement in one's day-to-day teaching, and formal evaluation to aid institutional decision-making. The latter can be undertaken at different levels — department, course committee, faculty, academic board, directorate, etc. — and is essentially the species of evaluation promoted since *Partnership in Validation* by the CNAA. According to how the latter is conceived and conducted it may go beyond the strictly instrumental function to encompass the concept of evaluation we have been particularly concerned to explore in this book: evaluation not only to serve managerial decision-making, but also to enhance professional and institutional growth and development. The way evaluation findings are treated, as we argued in the previous chapter, provides a clear indicator as to its potential. Where evaluation findings are accorded the finite status of objective fact, accepted and acted upon with little debate, they have far less potential for promoting such development than if they are treated as partial evidence or hypothesis in a continuing process of appraisal and modification. So far, in higher-education institutions we see a predominance of the view of the evaluation 'finding' as the terminal point — the 'product' view of evaluation — and little evidence of the 'process' view which accords all but the most self-evidently unchallengeable evaluation findings interim status and encourages varieties of interpretations of data by individuals and groups with different interests and perspectives before determining what decisions they indicate. In this view the evaluation process itself is seen as having as significant a potential for supporting development as the evaluation finding or product, provided that the process is collective and open.

The individual and the institution

One of the central tensions highlighted by formal evaluation is that between individual professional autonomy and corporate institutional interest. In concentrating in this book on evaluation as a collective and public activity we would not wish to be seen as denying the necessity for and potency of private self-evaluation. Without individual commitment, self-awareness and self-critique, collective acts in an arena like education have little validity. We have taken the primacy of such self-appraisal for granted. But since in parts of the British educational system — particularly perhaps in universities — this may be seen as the *only* valid form of curricular evaluation, we have also felt it desirable to stress its limitations — not merely in the obvious sense that each person's capacity to be critical of his own work, or to be aware of alternative ways of undertaking it, may be limited, but arising in a more fundamental way from our assumptions about what a course or a curriculum is. It is not a collection of isolated teaching acts, but an interdependent network of activities placed in what is claimed to be a meaningful juxtaposition, in pursuit of an explicit set of general goals set by the institution. Moreover, *a student's* version of a course — arguably the one that matters most — is the product of a variety of experiences and encounters over a period of time. Their impact is longitudinally cumulative, and latitudinally penetrating. Course evaluation has to be more than a collection of individual self-evaluations: it has to explore what these separate activities add up to, the relationship between them, their coherence, their consistency, their cumulative impact on and meaning for the student. Course evaluation thus is necessarily collective: an attribute usually accepted for course planning.

We are concerned, however, at the extent to which institutional structures and professional ideologies may present individual autonomy and collective obligation as mutually exclusive. Pursued as an end in itself the former can restrict genuine professional development and provide a cloak not only for poor teaching and ill-conceived courses but also for the abuse of power by some which in the end reduces the actual autonomy of others. Conversely, pursued to excess the doctrine of collectivism in educational institutions may stifle initiative, creativity and the element of idiosyncrasy and unpredictability essential to truly engaged teaching. We fear that while some institutions or departments may have taken autonomy to irresponsible extremes, others may have so regulated individual professional conduct in the pursuit of collectivism that the result can be just as damaging to the quality of teaching and learning. We would expect the matter of *balance* here to be central to an institution's debate about evaluation:

☐ What is the most productive balance and relationship of public/ formal and private/informal educational evaluations? What are the strengths and limitations of aspiring to holism and coherence in course design and cohesiveness in staff relationships? In what areas might individual initiative be particularly productive? And for what purpose is professional cooperation particularly useful? At what points might each become counter-productive in terms of the quality of the student's learning experiences? (Alexander, 1980b, p. 187)   ☐

Evaluation and management

Courses do not proceed in a vacuum; they are not merely proposals and classroom events: they are derived from and embedded in decision-making contexts. If asked to justify an educational institution's buildings, resources, management structures and procedures, administrative and technical services, most of us would assert that these all exist to further the central goals of the institution, namely to provide the highest quality of teaching and learning, and in certain institutions, research and the advancement of knowledge. There is little doubt that these contexts, (especially, in our view, the management/decision-making context) contribute significantly to the quality of teaching and learning. Moreover, unless educational management is conducted in as responsive and self-critical a manner as teaching is expected to be, there is limited potential for course improvement except in those fairly unimportant areas which remain uninfluenced by management. Thus if courses are to be evaluated, so must be course and institutional management and decision-making frameworks and procedures; if teachers are to be evaluated, so must be managers.

The model of course evaluation currently emerging from the CNAA appears to rest on a view of education and educational management as distinct and separable, in that it envisages one group — course and institutional management — evaluating the activities of another group — students and teachers (see CNAA, 1980 and 1981). Procedures for course evaluation which exempt major sectors of the institution which contribute significantly to the quality of these courses have little constructive use.

We have discussed concepts and practices of management in large educational institutions, and have suggested a fundamental problem in comparing certain approaches to management and the nature of the activities being 'managed', stemming pre-eminently from the failure of the former to accommodate the value-divergence and exploration basic to the educational process.

We argued that the now very familiar bureaucratic/mechanistic institutional structures, though often introduced partly in furtherance of the 'democratic' claim and partly in pursuit of administrative efficiency, may be neither democratic nor particularly efficient. Such structures can be singularly inappropriate vehicles for the relatively open-ended, flexible and critical debate which progress in as value-laden an area as education requires, and they may illustrate a general incapacity to cope with change.

Just how deficient in this regard some of our most august institutions can be was well illustrated by the McCabe affair at Cambridge University. Here, as the transcript of the Senate debate makes clear (Cambridge University, 1981), the matter of McCabe's failure to gain tenure was in itself less of an issue than the capacity of the English faculty to manage its affairs. The familiar symptoms re-emerge: the assumption of consensus, of single shared truths about a particular educational activity (the teaching of English); the suppression of dissent; the concentration of power in the hands of a minority; the lack of mutual accountability relationships; and above all the inability to countenance, let alone to accommodate, new ideas and critiques of the activities at the heart of the institution's work: that supposed hallmark of a university, intellectual curiosity and vitality, was acceptable only so long as it was directed away from the ideas and practices of the university itself as an organization.

We encapsulated some of these problems in our contrast between an 'epistemology of management' and our 'epistemology of evaluation'. However, we do not see management and educational evaluation as inherently incompatible: the theorizing institution can be, and in our knowledge frequently is, also an efficiently-managed institution. The problem is the relative inappropriateness of concepts of management applied in some institutions and we feel that these merit urgent appraisal, perhaps in the first instance as part of those institutions' evaluation programmes.

Evaluation: appendage or central activity?

Educational evaluation is the invocation and use of criteria and evidence as a basis for making judgements about educational endeavours; such judgements may be used to inform decisions about the subsequent direction of those endeavours. Our work in Charlesford and Enlands, like others' elsewhere, was in a distinct area of institutional life labelled 'evaluation', yet by our definition of the word many other sorts of institutional activity are equally 'evaluative' though they do not use that label. Apart from the 'hidden', informal evaluation fundamental to the teaching act, which we discussed in chapter one, much institutional decision-making is grounded in evaluation of a more deliberate sort: appointments and promotions of staff, course development, internal validation of course proposals, day-to-day institutional management activities. All these are clearly and overtly evaluative activities yet may be undertaken with little consciousness that the sorts of questions we have raised about formal, named 'evaluation' apply equally to them. What are the criteria for evaluating an applicant for appointment or promotion, for instance? How comprehensive and valid is the evidence? What is the extent of distortion of the judgements by personal or sectional values and interests on the part of those judging the application? How, in essence, can x claim to 'know' that y is the best candidate for a post? The same questions can be asked about a wide variety of judgements and decisions made in the course of the day-to-day conduct of an institution's affairs.

Frequently, such judgements and decisions may have consequences for individuals and groups at least as serious as those resulting from activities formally carrying the 'evaluation' label and consequently subject to the sorts of safeguards and restrictions illustrated by the Charlesford and Enlands evaluations. In our view it makes little sense to set up and carefully circumscribe formal evaluation procedures for certain aspects of an institution's work if the evaluations on which the greater part of the institution's decisions are based remain unexamined, (or more commonly, concealed beneath the cloak of confidentiality or hierarchical privilege), and if examined are manifestly inadequate as to their criterial and evidential bases.

However, where such evaluations emanate from outside an institution they do tend to be appraised in this way. Thus there is no shortage of critics of the judgements on which the CNAA external validation decisions are based; the process of institutional review by the CNAA is described (Ball, 1981) as 'impractical, unreal, impertinent, unprofessional'; the University Grants Committee is accused (Crequer, 1981) of basing its decisions on out-of-date information. In all such cases, though the word 'evaluation' is not used, it is the adequacy of the evaluation on which the decision is based — as to criteria, focus, evidence and so on — as much as the decision itself which is subject to criticism. Such sensitivity to the evaluative dimension of decision-making ought to apply with equal force to decisions made *within* institutions: how many institutional decisions and judgements are 'impractical, unreal, impertinent, unprofessional'?

In our 'theorizing institution', then, it is not merely courses, students, teaching and learning which are subject to evaluation and debate, but the evaluative process itself, wherever it occurs in such a way as to significantly influence individuals' situations, especially in teaching and in management. Perhaps the difficulties facing educational institutions in the early 1980s will at last alert people to the pervasiveness and frequent inadequacy of the evaluative process. In universities, for example, facing the now inevitable loss of staff and courses, judgements will have to be made about their relative merits. Who will make these judgements? By what right? Using what criteria? Adducing what evidence? With what right of reply? With what possibility for alternative perspectives and judgements? Already it is suggested in some universities that the only fair procedure for determining compulsory redundancies is to apply promotion criteria and procedures. This, of course, does not make the redundancy judgement more valid: it simply compounds the relative crudity of the criteria and evidential bases for the promotion judgement. Perhaps faced with evaluation in this form academics will develop a belated consciousness of the centrality of evaluation to life in educational institutions, will recognize it as a process which extends well beyond the hitherto narrow usage of 'evaluation' as denoting assessing students' performance on courses, and will seek to render more explicit and defensible some of the many evaluations on which decisions are based which affect the lives of themselves and their students. The motivation may be self-preservation rather than the improvement of institutional thought and practice, but it may achieve the same shift of evaluation from wings to centre stage in the interests of institutional development.

But we would not wish this example to seem to suggest that consciousness of evaluation should be restricted to only those manifestations of it which threaten teachers and lecturers. All significant activity in educational institutions is evaluative, and we would expect the theorizing institution to be concerned to test the adequacy of the judgements which inform teaching and course development as carefully as those which affect staff careers.

Is formal evaluation redundant?

Does a consciousness of teaching-as-evaluation and management-as-evaluation render redundant separate formal evaluation procedures like those at Enlands and Charlesford? This might seem a logical consequence in a situation where an institution's full range of judgements — pedagogical, managerial, financial, academic — are undertaken with the sort of sensitivity to their epistemological and value dimensions, and with the sort of safeguards for the integrity of the judgemental process and the rights of individuals and groups that we advocate for formal evaluation. Certainly to call one activity 'evaluation' and others 'teaching', or 'course development' or 'internal validation', or 'management' seems positively to invite those concerned with the latter activities to ignore the judgemental sensitivity, complexity and challengeability of their work, and to argue 'You evaluate, and leave us to get on with the job of teaching/managing/developing courses . . .'

However, we have no illusions about the Utopian character of the theorizing institution, and about the currently limited extent of evaluation-consciousness in many of the facets of institutional life listed above. Indeed, we can anticipate our argument being used to justify inaction: 'who needs something called "evaluation" if we're all evaluators now?' (A by no means hypothetical deduction: we both encountered it in our institutions and continue to do so.) In such circumstances the formal evaluation process can fulfil a vital function in moving the institution to a more genuine and pervasive evaluation-consciousness. We believe there to be an inevitability or inexorability about this for, as we have shown, formal evaluations have a way of challenging and disturbing assumptions and practices beyond those they are established to cover. There are many convincing parallels to our experience here, where the apparently limited formal procedure gradually extends its influence to reach basic habits of thought and practice untouched by the pseudo-challenge of professional autonomy. External validation requirements, for example, have altered the consciousness of many staff in public sector higher education institutions about course development and pedagogy: here the external requirement spurs an internal response which is considerably more profound than the merely procedural (Alexander and Wormald, 1982; Alexander and Gent, 1982). Or the recent legislation covering school prospectuses, coupled with LEA 'school review' requirements may force school staff collectively to examine their purposes and arrangements to an extent and depth impossible during the expansionist and complacent 1960s.

However, there must be no illusions either about the extent to which the educational crisis of the early 1980s works against evaluation as well as for it. 'Rationalization' may dictate a still more restricted concept of management, a greater degree of centralization (Lindop, 1981), a tendency to exclude educational quality from criteria of efficiency. Intellectual ferment may be replaced by tension and conflict between different interest groups, and the openness to external ideas and influences may be replaced by a growing introversion (Briggs, 1981). A virtual freeze on promotions and appointments, the absence of new blood, will exacerbate those problems (Williams, 1981), and those in positions of power may feel increasingly relieved of the responsibility to explicate and justify their assumptions and actions.

There are many routes to the self-evaluating institution, to ways of keeping open the educational debate at all levels during a period when survival may seem the only imperative. The formal evaluation programme is one of them: it provides a modest and workable basis for development. However, we would commend as a first priority the appraisal of those evaluations on which the existing basic practices of the institution depend — teaching, assessment, course development, management and decision-making — in the context of which the word 'evaluation' may be seldom, if ever, used.

GLOSSARY

This glossary is provided on the assumption that in a book aimed at a rather diverse readership there will be some terms with a specialist, stipulative or local meaning on which some readers will welcome clarification.

Accountability   The condition of being held answerable or culpable for the quality and efficiency of one's actions, individually or collectively, by and to other persons or bodies, either external to one's work-setting ('public' accountability) or within the same setting (such as colleagues, managers, students, academic boards etc.).

Action research   A mode of inquiry which reports back to 'actors' (for instance, teachers, lecturers, course administrators) in a given (educational) setting data collected on the basis of issues and concerns defined by them. Action research's aspiration is to improve practice through increasing the actors' knowledge of their performance and interrelationships and of the constraints and contexts within which they work.

B.Ed.   Bachelor of Education degree. (1) The Initial B.Ed. combines academic study with teacher preparation, and the degree award includes Qualified Teacher Status (QTS) to allow direct entry into that profession. The first B.Eds, validated by universities, were awarded in 1968; now (1982) the majority are validated by CNAA (q.v.). They replaced the earlier majority route into state schools (other than by non-teaching degrees with or without PCGE), the Teacher's Certificate. (2) The In-service B.Ed. is taken by experienced teachers, usually those who trained before the Initial B.Ed. qualification became available. It tends to be more exclusively professional in orientation and, of course, assumes the student's basic competence as a teacher.

Behavioural objectives   The point of departure, in theory at least, for the mainstream tradition in educational evaluation. Educational aims are refined into a set of observable and measurable behaviours by which the student will demonstrate his learning. These provide the basis both for a structured and systematized approach to the planning of a sequence of learning experiences and the foci for evaluation. The task of the evaluator or teacher becomes that of devising and administering instruments for measuring the extent to which each of these constituent behavioural objectives has been achieved. The theoretical and practical objections to this model are numerous and substantial, and the debate has occupied many on both sides of the Atlantic. However, many statements on course or programme evaluation (e.g. in proposals to the CNAA) put forward arrangements on evaluation and adopt the behavioural objectives evaluation model apparently with no awareness of how contentious it is, or how limited are the claims which can be made for it (or, for that matter, for any single doctrine of evaluation, whether quantitative or qualitative).

Binary system/principle   The current organization of British higher education, strongly confirmed by the Robbins Report of 1963, into a relatively autonomous university sector and a 'public' sector controlled by LEAs.

Collaboration   As a research methodology collaboration acknowledges the establishing of reciprocity with practitioners in the process of identification of issues and concerns which become the subject of shared inquiries. The person qualified and experienced in research and development provides advice and technical assistance to help practitioners achieve success in their inquiries. The researcher, as collaborator, would be sympathetic to and in critical dialogue with the aspirations of the practitioners.

Colleges of education   Formerly called 'training colleges' (a label still erroneously applied). Institutions within the higher education sector set up specifically to train teachers. Since the re-organization of teacher education in the 1970s few purely teacher training ('monotechnic') institutions remain. Of the colleges that continued after the reorganization, the majority have been re-named colleges or institutes of higher education, having diversified the range of their courses.

Colleges/Institutes of higher education   The sixty-two colleges/institutes within public-sector higher education offering courses of a diverse nature, including first and higher degrees in education, the humanities, social sciences and social services. Some incorporate a substantial proportion of vocational and non-vocational further education provision.

Concurrent (B.Ed.).   An arrangement of the B.Ed. course by which academic study is interspersed with professionally orientated study and school-based teaching practice. Contrasted with a *consecutive* arrangement where such vocational orientation follows after academic study.

Council for National Academic Awards (CNAA)   Established in 1964, in response to recommendations of the Robbins Committee on Higher Education, to award degrees, diplomas and other qualifications in institutions other than universities, and to ensure that such awards are, in the words of the CNAA Royal Charter, 'comparable in standards to those conferred by universities'. CNAA is now 'the largest single degree-awarding body in the United Kingdom and about one-third of all students who are studying for a degree in this country attend CNAA courses' (CNAA, 1979b). Associated institutions include polytechnics, colleges of education, colleges/institutes of higher education, art, music, technology, drama and other specialist areas. The 'public' sector is not exclusively CNAA validated — universities and various technical/professional/vocational councils and bodies are also involved — but at degree, diploma and higher-degree level CNAA predominates. (Its mode of operation is described and appraised in our text).

Courses/programmes/curricula   There is no agreed usage for these terms, which are frequently interchanged. However, we need to draw attention to two prevailing usages which conflict with each other and to note the considerable risk of confusion.

1 'Programme' frequently means in the USA what 'course' means in the terminology stipulated by the British CNAA (1979c, p. 43): i.e. the total body of regulations, timetabled activities, options, assessment procedures and so on leading to a given award such as B.A.

2 'Course' frequently means in the USA what 'course component' is defined as in CNAA parlance: i.e. a single, constituent part of an overall structure.

3 'Programme' in CNAA parlance is an individual student's route through a course structure, his possibly unique collection of options, etc. Thus: (CNAA) student x's *programme* on the B.A. *course* at institution y consists of *course components* a, b, c and d. or: (USA) student x's route or sequence on the B.A. *programme* at institution y consists of *courses* a, b, c and d.

4 The range of definitions of 'curriculum' is considerably wider than course/programme and we cannot enumerate them here. They range from (narrow) a printed syllabus indicating official *intentions* to (broad) the full collection of *intended* and *actual* learning experiences.

Department of Education and Science (DES) A branch of central government controlling expenditure, evolving and implementing policy and monitoring the activities of schools, further and higher education, science, museums, libraries, nationally-owned centres for the arts. Incorporates ministers, permanent civil servants and HM Inspectors of Education under the control of the Secretary of State for Education and Science.

Diploma in Higher Education (Dip.H.E.) A two-year qualification currently offered in at least twenty-three public sector institutions of higher education. Recommended in James Report (q.v.) as an alternative means of entry to and study in higher education, but subsequently approved on condition that normal matriculation qualifications had been gained. Frequently provides 'base' for several alternative degree courses (e.g. B.A., B.Sc., B.Ed.)

Feedback schedule A device, usually in closed questionnaire or checklist form, to enable teachers/lecturers to receive comments or ratings on their courses and classroom performance from their students.

Formative/summative evaluation A distinction made by Scriven (1967) between *formative* evaluation undertaken during the development of a course/programme to be fed back into the development process, and *summative* evaluation undertaken after the course/programme is completed.

Her Majesty's Inspectors/Inspectorate of Schools (HMI) A branch of the Department of Education and Science which provides advice on the basis of maintaining an overview of educational developments at every level of the system down to individual classrooms and schools. While serving as the 'eyes and ears' of the DES, HMI have also enjoyed — and guarded — a degree of professional autonomy from successive governments and ministers.

Houghton Committee/Award (1974) A study of the pay of public-sector teachers which resulted in the 'Houghton Award' of 1975. It included recommendations on staffing, gradings and hierarchies as well as on their remuneration, and thus had an impact on institutions' organizational structures.

Illuminative evaluation A phrase coined by Parlett and Hamilton (1972) to denote, as an alternative methodology to objectives-referenced educational measurement, techniques more akin to those of anthropological fieldwork: observation, interview, 'progressive focusing' on, and defining of, issues as they emerge in the course of study rather than in advance.

James Report Report of Committee of Inquiry into Teacher Education and Training, set up by central government in 1970, and reporting in 1972. Introduced idea of Dip.H.E., and the 'three cycle' notion of teacher education — (1) personal education, (2) pre-service professional training and induction into teaching, (3) in-service education and training.

Literary modes of evaluation Exemplified in the study at the end of chapter 3. They offer an alternative methodology to those in the social sciences whether quantitative-grounded psychometric or anthropological. Methodology hard to pin down, but basically premissed on the argument that the artist/writer/literary critic can provide perspectives on and insights into educational events of greater richness and subtlety than traditional evaluation methods and having as strong a 'truth' claim. Key exponents are Eisner (1979), Walker (1980), Pick and Walker (1975), Mann (1978).

Local Education Authority (LEA) Branch of local government responsible under the 1944 Education Act for ensuring the provision of primary, secondary and further/higher education, facilities for recreation and leisure, etc. in its area. Constituted of permanent officers, educational advisers etc., under the control of an education committee including elected and co-opted members. Higher education, under the 'binary' system, is conducted in both universities, which are independent of local authority control, and LEA-controlled institutions such as polytechnics, colleges/institutes of higher education.

Matrix management A form of internal management of large educational institutions, characteristic of polytechnics, and, more recently, of colleges of education and colleges/institutes of higher education, wherein task and resource concerns and responsibilities are differentiated and controlled by different bodies rather than integrated under unified control. Thus, for example, one axis of management might control total courses (B.A., B.Sc., B.Ed.), and be manifested in the work of course committees. The other axis would be responsible for providing the academic content of such courses according to the pre-specified overall course framework, and for staffing them; typically this role is filled by departments.

Participant observation   A method of inquiry which requires the researcher both to be present at and to some extent engaged in the activities being studied. The participation is intended to provide a greater depth of understanding, enabling the observer to 'get inside' the actors' perspective, than detached, non-participant observation.

Personal/professional   A distinction, basic to all recent teacher education, between that part of a course which provides a higher education 'for its own sake', and that part which concentrates on the specific knowledge and skills required for the teaching task. Sometimes the division is termed academic/professional, or even education/training.

Portrayal evaluation   Term used loosely to indicate a style of evaluation which aims to present an image or description of educational events 'as they are', or as they are perceived by an external portrayer, rather than as they are claimed to be by those with a vested interest in presenting them in a particular way. The emphasis is on educational *processes*, rather than on intentions or outcomes, though it can also encompass these, and the 'subjectivity' inherent in all portrayal is deemed necessary and valuable rather than something to be avoided.

Polytechnics   Thirty 'public' sector, LEA controlled higher education institutions, mostly formed as a result of merging existing colleges (e.g. of art, commerce, technology and education), established after a government White Paper of 1966. They offer a wide range of full-time, part-time, sandwich and mixed-mode degree, diploma and other courses, initially mostly vocationally-oriented but increasingly covering a full spread of academic areas and purposes.

Postgraduate Certificate in Education (PGCE)   One-year course of teacher preparation, leading to the postgraduate certificate and qualified teacher status, for those who already possess a degree or equivalent qualification. PGCE places are shared roughly 50:50 between university departments/schools of education and public-sector institutions of higher education. Unlike the B.Ed. degree, university, rather than CNAA, validation still predominates in the public sector.

Pre-ordinate research/evaluation   Inquiry taking as its point of reference objectives, criteria or methods which are set before the work has begun. Pre-ordinate evaluation is characteristically concerned with establishing the extent to which a course's pre-specified objectives have been achieved. Contrast with 'responsive' (q.v.).

Psychometry/psychometric Methods (here usually for ascertaining levels of pupil/student performance or ability) based on the assumption that mental attributes are measurable and hence will yield quantifiable data.

Qualitative v. quantitative evaluation A debate centring (1) on the reliability of particular evaluation methods, (2) their appropriateness for appraising the complexities of educational events. Arguments for qualitative evaluation (e.g. literary modes) have generally arisen as a direct response to the perceived inadequacy of quantitative methods (e.g. psychometry, closed survey techniques) in respect of (1) and (2), and especially in response to what critics perceive as some quantitative methods' tendency to distort, or greatly oversimplify educational 'reality'. However, while quantitative methods produce 'results' in the form of firm statements, figures and conclusions, qualitative methods tend to highlight impressions, complexities, alternative perceptions and explanations. Inevitably, therefore, many decision-makers in education, particularly at senior management level, find quantitative methods more useful for the purpose of informing decisions about resource allocation.

Questionnaires A set of questions on a given topic addressed to each member of a sample of a given population. Questionnaires can invite respondents to select from several pre-specified responses the one which most closely matches their views ('closed', 'fixed choice' questionnaires), or they can invite 'open' responses, putting no restrictions on the response. The questions themselves can range from the very general to the highly specific: thus the set of highly specific questions with closed responses is more straightforward to analyse and yields quantifiable data and is less likely to meet objections of researcher/analyst 'intervention' at the analysis stage. On the other hand, the respondent's views are strictly circumscribed by what the questionnaire-designer deems as the significant questions and the range of appropriate answers.

Responsive evaluation Style of evaluation postulated by Stake (e.g. 1975, 1976) as alternative to the then dominant pre-ordinate quantitative modes. Where 'pre-ordinate evaluators know what they are looking for and design the study so as to find it, responsive studies are organized round phenomena encountered — often unexpectedly — along the way' (Stake, 1976). Responsive evaluation anticipates idiosyncrasy, unpredictability, and the uniqueness of individuals' experiences in educational settings. These form the basis both for the issues studied and the methods used.

Sampling   Statistical pre-selection from a total population, of individual cases deemed representative of significant elements and characteristics of that population and of the proportions in which they occur.

Schools Council for the Curriculum and Examinations   Established by central government in 1964 as the major national agency for curriculum development but also as being committed to respecting the autonomy of teachers and schools in such matters. Took over several Nuffield projects, steered debates on school examinations, and instituted major programme of curriculum renewal through funded projects based at colleges and universities, producing reports and/or teacher/pupil materials which were marketed commercially. Its mode of operation has recently been replaced by one which encourages less centralization, greater local initiative and teacher involvement. Now (1982) under threat from central government.

Social Science Research Council (SSRC)   One of five research councils allocated funds by the government Treasury. The SSRC funds research in the social sciences, history, geography and education.

Unit   A component of a course (q.v.) identified by a distinctive title, syllabus, objectives, content and assessment procedures, but planned as equivalent in terms of length, level of difficulty, assessment weighting, etc. to other units so as to permit maximum flexibility in student choice within and sometimes across courses.

Validation   Literally, the process of making valid, ratifying, confirming. In higher education it denotes the activities of validating bodies such as universities or the CNAA in declaring valid (1) a course of study leading to an award, (2) the currency of the award itself. Validation is of one body by another but can also be 'internal', often as a preliminary stage in a process culminating in the successful 'external' validation and operationalizing of a new course.

Weaver Report   Report of a study of group, chaired by Sir Toby Weaver, on the government of colleges of education, published in 1966. It recommended the reconstitution of governing bodies and the establishment of academic boards.

REFERENCES

Adams, E. (1980), 'The Ford Teaching Project', in Stenhouse, L. (ed.), *Curriculum Development and Research in Action,* London, Heinemann. **10**

Adelman, C. (1980), 'Some dilemmas of institutional evaluation and their relationship to pre-conditions and procedures', *Studies in Educational Evaluation*, vol. 6, Oxford, Pergamon, pp. 165–83. **15**

Adelman, C. (1981a), 'On first hearing', in Adelman, C. (ed.), *Uttering, Muttering*, London, Grant McIntyre. **169**

Adelman, C. (1981b), 'Knowledgeable users', in Fox, T. (ed.), *Evaluation and Policy Formation*, Madison, University of Wisconsin. **47**

Adelman, C. and Alexander, R. J. (1981), 'Who wants to know that? Aspects of institutional self-evaluation', in Oxtoby, R. (ed.), *Higher Education at the Crossroads*, Guildford, SRHE. **3**

Adelman, C. and Gibbs, I. (1979), *A Study of Student Choice in the Context of Institutional Change: Final Report to DES*, reprinted in *Collected Original Resources in Education* (Carfax), vol. 4, no. 1, 1980. **12**

Alexander, R. J. (1978a), *CNAA and Course Evaluation*, paper to CNAA Committee for Education, CNAA (mimeo). **3**

Alexander, R. J. (1978b), 'Setting up an internal evaluation', in Collier, K.G. (ed.), *Evaluating the New B.Ed.*, Guildford, SRHE. **3**

Alexander, R. J. (1978c), 'An internal evaluation: appraisal and speculations', in Collier, K. G. (ed.), *Evaluating the New B.Ed.*, Guildford, SRHE. **3**

Alexander, R. J. (1979), 'What is a course? Curriculum models and CNAA validation', *Journal of Further and Higher Education*, vol. 3, no. 1. **13, 16, 17, 156, 158**

Alexander, R. J. (1980a), 'Towards a conceptual framework for school-focused INSET', *British Journal of In-service Education*, vol. 6, no. 3. **11, 179**

Alexander, R. J. (1980b), 'The evaluation of advanced in-service courses for teachers: the challenge to providers', *British Journal of Teacher Education*, vol. 6, no. 3. **3, 25, 174, 185**

Alexander, R. J. and Harris, P. (1977), *The Evaluation of New Courses in a College of Education*, SSRC/Manchester Polytechnic. Reprinted in *Collected Original Resources in Education*, vol. 5, no. 3 (1981). **3, 12**

Alexander, R. J. and Wormald, E. (1982), 'Validation in teacher education: expectations, criteria and processes', in Church, C. H. (ed.), *Practice and Perspectives in Validation*, Guildford, SRHE. **12, 15, 154, 190**

Alexander, R. J., Billing, D. and Gent, B. (1980), *Partnership and Standards: Validation and Evaluation,* paper to CNAA *Partnership in Validation* Working Party, CNAA (mimeo). **3**

Alexander, R. J. and Gent, B. (1982), 'Internal validation in higher education institutions: characteristics, problems and justifications', in Church, C. H. (ed.), *Practice and Perspectives in Validation*, Guildford, SRHE. **13, 190**

Anderson, S. B., Ball, S. and Murphy, R. T. (1975), *Encyclopaedia of Educational Evaluation,* San Francisco, Jossey-Bass. **164**

Ball, C. J. E. (1981), 'The advancement of education, learning and the arts', Thames Polytechnic Annual Lecture, June 1981 (mimeo). **14, 16, 17, 188**

Bailey, F. G. (1977), *Morality and Expediency: The Folk Lore of Academic Politics*, Oxford, Blackwell. **155**

Barnes, J. A. (1979), *Who Shall Know What?*, London, Penguin. **15, 154**

Becher, A. R., Hewton, E., Simons, H. and Squires, G. (1976), *Making the Best of It*, (report from the Nuffield Foundation Group for Research and Innovation in Higher Education), Nuffield Foundation. **11**

Becher, A. R. and Kogan, M. (1980), *Process and Structure in Higher Education,* London, Heinemann Educational Books.

Becher, A. and Maclure, S. (1978), *Accountability in Education,* Slough, NFER. **17**

Becker, H. S. (1970), *Sociological Work: Method and Substance*, Chicago, Aldine. **16**

Bellow, S. (1971), *Mr Sammler's Planet,* London, Penguin. **167**

Bennis, W. G., Benne, K., Chin, R. and Corey, K. (1976), *The Planning of Change*, Holt, Rinehart Winston. **173, 176**

Berg, B. and Oestergren, B. (1977), *Innovations and Innovation Processes in Higher Education*, National Board of Universities and Colleges, Stockholm. **20, 22**

Bernbaum, G. (1975), 'Countesthorpe College', in Harris, A., Lawn, M., Prescott, W. (eds), *Curriculum Innovation*, London/Milton Keynes, Croom Helm/Open University Press. **176**

Bioletti, P. (1981), 'How shall we know what they are telling us? An attempt to gather numerical information from responses to open questions', *Evaluation Newsletter*, vol. 5, no. 2. **170**

Biott, C. (1979), 'The insider as evaluator: practical issues in a college context', *Evaluation Newsletter*, vol. 3, no. 1. **170**

Bloom. B. S., Hastings, J. T. and Madaus, G. F. (1971), *Handbook of Formative and Summative Evaluation of student learning*, New York, McGraw-Hill. **7, 165**

Braskamp, L. A. (1980), 'The role of evaluation in faculty development', *Studies in Higher Education*, vol. 5, no. 1, March. **16, 18, 19, 134.**

Briggs, A. (1981), 'Less ferment but more conflict', *Times Higher Education Supplement*, no. 467. **190**

Burns, T. and Stalker, G. M. (1966), *The Management of Innovation*, London, Tavistock. **154, 158, 173**

Cambridge, University of (1981), 'Report of meeting of the Senate to discuss the state of the English Faculty', *Cambridge University Reporter*, no. 5108, 18 February 1981. **186**

Chambers, P. (ed.) (1981), *Making INSET Work: Myth Reality?*, Papers from the Curriculum and Educational Development In-service Network, Bradford College. **11**

Church, C. H. (ed.) (1982), *Practice and Perspectives in Validation*, Guildford, SRHE. **7**

Cohen, D. and Garet, M. (1975), 'Reforming educational policy with applied social research', *Harvard Educational Review*, vol. 45, no. 1. **130**

Council for National Academic Awards (1975), *Partnership in Validation*, London, CNAA (mimeo). **13**

Council for National Academic Awards (1979a), *Developments in Partnership in Validation*, London, CNAA. **13, 133**

Council for National Academic Awards (1979b), *The Council: Its Place in British Higher Education*, London, CNAA. **193**

Council for National Academic Awards (1979c), *Principles and Regulations for the Award of the Council's First Degrees and Diploma of Higher Education*, London, CNAA. **193**

Council for National Academic Awards (1980), *Institutional Reviews: Notes for the Guidance of Institutions*, London, CNAA (mimeo). **15, 133, 138, 186**

Council for National Academic Awards (1981), *A Note of Guidance on Critical Appraisal of Courses*, London, CNAA (mimeo). **15, 186**

Crequer, N. (1981), 'UGC cuts based on out-of-date information', *Times Higher Educational Supplement*, no. 457. **188**

CRITE (1976–9) CRITE/SRHE (1979–) (Committee for Research in Teacher Education/Society for Research into Higher Education) *Evaluation Newsletter*. **12, 56**

Cronbach, L. J. (1963), 'Course improvement through evaluation', *Teachers College Record*, no. 64. **164**

Davis, M. C. (1980), 'The CNAA as a validating agency', in Billing, D. E. (ed.), *Indicators of Performance*, Guildford, SRHE. **157**

Department of Education and Science (1966), *Report of the Study Group on the Government of Colleges of Education* (Weaver Report), London, HMSO. **53, 147, 148**

Department of Education and Science (1972a), *Teacher Education and Training* (James Report), London, HMSO. **31, 52, 149**

Department of Education and Science (1972b), *Education: A Framework for Expansion*, London, HMSO. **33**

Department of Education and Science (1977), *Education in Schools: A Consultative Document*, London, HMSO. **10**

Department of Education and Science (1980), *A Framework for the School Curriculum: Proposals for Consultation,* London, HMSO. **10**

Department of Education and Science (1981), *The School Curriculum*, London, HMSO. **10**

Dressel, P. (1976), *Handbook of Academic Evaluation*, San Francisco, Jossey-Bass. **7, 16, 19**

Eisner, E. W. (1967), 'Educational objectives: help or hindrance?', *School Review*, vol. 75. **18**

Eisner, E. W. (1969), 'Instructional and expressive objectives', in Popham, W. J., Eisner, E. W., Sullivan, H. J., Tyler, L. L., *Instructional Objectives*, Chicago, Rand McNally. **18, 166**

Eisner, E. W. (1979), *The Educational Imagination*, London, Macmillan. **18, 101, 110, 164, 195**

Elliot, J. (1976), 'Preparing teachers for classroom accountability', *Education for Teaching*, no. 100. **169**

Elliott, J. (1977), 'Conceptualizing relationships between research/evaluation procedures and in-service education', *British Journal of In-service Education*, vol. 4, no. 1. **170**

Elliott, J. and Adelman, C. (1975), 'Teacher education for curriculum reform: an interim report of the Ford Teaching Project', *British Journal of Teacher Education*, vol. 1, no. 1. **10**

Elliott, J. and Adelman, C. (1976), 'Innovation at the classroom level: a case study of the Ford Teaching Project', Course E203, *Curriculum Design and Development*, Unit 28, Milton Keynes, Open University Press. **10, 134**

Eraut, M. (1976), 'Some recent evaluation studies of curriculum projects: a review', in Tawney, D. (ed.), *Curriculum Evaluation Today: Trends and Implications,* London, Macmillan. **1**

Eraut, M., Goad, L. and Smith, G. (1975), *The Analysis of Curriculum Materials*, Education Area Occasional Paper no. 2, University of Sussex. **13**

Eraut, M., Connors, B. and Hewton, E. (1981), *Training in Curriculum Development and Educational Technology in Higher Education*, Research into Higher Education Monographs, Guildford, SRHE. **12**

Fletcher, C. and Adelman, C. (1981), 'Collaboration as a research process', *Community Education Journal*, no. 1, Coventry. **115**

Flood-Page, C. (1977), *Student Evaluation of Teaching: The American Experience*, Guildford, SRHE. **7**

Furumark, A. M. (1979), *Activity Evaluation in Higher Education: A Swedish Project*, Stockholm, National Board of Universities and Colleges, Research and Development Division (mimeo). **16**

Furumark, A. M. (1980), 'Institutional self-evaluation in Sweden', paper presented at the Fifth General Conference of OECD Programme on Institutional Management in Higher Education, Paris (mimeo). **20–2**

Gagné, R. (1972), 'Curriculum research and the promotion of learning', in Tyler, R., Gagné, R., Scriven, M., *Perspectives of Curriculum Evaluation,* AERA monograph, Chicago, Rand McNally. **165**

Gibson, R. (1981), 'Curriculum criticism: misconceived theory, ill-advised practice', *Cambridge Journal of Education*, vol. 11, no. 3. **111**

Gouldner, A. W. (1954), *Patterns of Industrial Bureaucracy.*, New York, Free Press. **154**

Habermas, J. (1970), *Toward a Rational Society*, New York, Beacon Press. **169**

Hamilton, D., Jenkins, D., King, G., MacDonald, B. and Parlett, M. (eds) (1977), *Beyond the Numbers Game*, London, Macmillan Educational. **164**

Harding, H. (1978), 'Harding replies to Hencke over college closures', *Education*, 29 December. **31**

Harding, H. (1979), 'Dull truth transmuted to fool's gold', *Education*, 5 January. **31, 48**

Havelock, R. (1977), *Planning for Innovation through Dissemination and Utilization of Knowledge*, Ann Arbor, University of Michigan Press. **22**

Hencke, D. (1978), *Colleges in Crisis*, London, Penguin. **31**

Heywood, J. (1977), *Assessment in Higher Education*, London, Wiley. **7**

Hoste, H. R. (1975), 'Evaluation in the college content', *Education for Teaching*, vol. 97. **145**

Hoste, H. R. (1981), 'Course appraisal using semantic differential scales', *Educational Studies*, October. **12**

Hoste, H. R. (1982), 'Curriculum evaluation using a seminar interaction analysis schedule', *Journal of Further and Higher Education*, June. **12**

House, E. R. (1973), *School Evaluation: The Politics and Process*, Berkeley, McCutchan. **161**

Inglis, F. (1975), *Ideology and the Imagination*, Cambridge, Cambridge University Press. **18**

Inner London Education Authority (1977), *Keeping the School under Review*, ILEA. **10**

Kemmis, S., Atkin, R. and Wright, E. (1978), *How do Students Learn?*, CARE Occasional Paper no. 5, University of East Anglia. **7**

Kerr, E., Billing, D. E., Bethel, D., Gent, B. B., Webster, H., Wyatt, J. F. and Oakeshott, A. M. (1980), 'CNAA validation and course evaluation: implications of the *Partnership in Validation* proposals', *Evaluation Newsletter*, vol. 4, no. 1. **13**

Kliebard, H. M. (1974), 'The development of certain key issues in the

United States', in Taylor, P. H. and Johnson, M. (eds), *Curriculum Development: A Comparative Study*, Slough, NFER. **18**

Lane, M. (1975), *Design for Degrees: New Degree Courses under the CNAA 1964–74*, London, Macmillan. **157**

Lewin, K. (1948), *Resolving Social Conflicts*, New York, Harper & Row. **22, 173**

Lindop, N. (1981), 'Seeking a middle poly way', *Times Higher Education Supplement*, no. 467. **190**

Lortie, D. C. (1973), 'Rational decision-making: is it possible today?', in House, E. R. (ed.), *School Evaluation: The Politics and Process*, Berkeley, McCutchan. **156**

Lubasz, H. (1981), 'Popper in Utopia', *Times Higher Education Supplement*, no. 477. **171**

Lynch, J. (1979), *The Reform of Teacher Education in the United Kingdom*, Guildford, SRHE. **149**

MacDonald, B. (1976a), 'Evaluation and the control of education', in Tawney, D. (ed.), *Curriculum Evaluation Today: Trends and Implications*, London, Macmillan. **55, 177**

MacDonald, B. (1976b), 'Who's afraid of evaluation?', *Education 3–13*, October 1976. **16**

MacDonald, B. (1981), 'Mandarines and lemons — the executive investment in program evaluation', paper presented at AERA symposium, Los Angeles (mimeo.) **162**

Mann, J. S. (1978), 'Curriculum criticism', in Willis, G. (ed.), *Qualitative Evaluation: Concepts and Cases in Curriculum Criticism*, Berkeley, McCutchan. **164**

Moodie, G. and Eustace, R. (1974), *Power and Authority in British Universities*, London, Allen & Unwin. **174**

Nixon, J. (1981), *A Teacher's Guide to Action Research*, London, Grant McIntyre. **10**

O'Neil, M. J. (1981), 'Nominal group technique: an evaluation data collection process', *Evaluation Newsletter*, vol. 5, no. 2. **170**

Parlett, M. and Hamilton, D. (1972), *Evaluation as Illumination: A New Approach to the Study of Innovatory Programmes*, CRES. Occasional Paper no. 9, Edinburgh. **55, 69, 164, 195**

Pick, C and Walker, R. (1975), *Other Rooms, Other Voices*, CARE, University of East Anglia. **195**

Pienkowski, A. E. and Cameron-Jones, M. (1980), 'Oliver's "Survey of Opinions about Education": a report on currency', *Evaluation Newsletter*, vol. 4, no. 2. ' **170**

Popham, W. J., Eisner, W. W., Sullivan, H. J. and Tyler, L. C. (1969), *Instructional Objectives*, AERA Monograph, Chicago, Rand McNally. **164**

Popper, K. R. (1972), *Conjectures and Refutations: The Growth of Scientific Knowledge*, London, Routledge & Kegan Paul. **167**

Powell, J. P., Connor, D. V. and Simmatt, C. (1980), 'Assessing the educational value of a construction project carried out by architecture students', *Evaluation Newsletter*, vol. 4, no. 1. **170**

Rein, M. (1976), *Social Science and Social Policy*, London, Penguin. **130**

Rippey, R. (1975), 'Student evaluations of professors: are they of value?' *Journal of Medical Education*, vol. 30, no. 10, October. **16, 19**

Salford Education Department (1977), *The Primary School Profile*, City of Salford (mimeo). **10**

Schensul, S. L. (1980), 'Anthropological fieldwork and sociopolitical change', *Social Problems*, vol. 28, no. 3. **115**

Schon, D. (1971), *Beyond the Stable State*, London, Penguin. **22, 173**

Schools Council (1981), *The Practical Curriculum*, Working Paper 70, London, Methuen Educational. **10**

Scriven, M. (1967), 'The methodology of evaluation', in Tyler, R., Gagné, R., Scriven, M., *Perspectives of Curriculum Evaluation*. AERA Monograph, Chicago, Rand McNally. **54, 194**

Selznick, P. (1948), *TVA and the Grass Roots*, Berkeley, University of California Press. **153**

Simons, H. (1980), 'Towards a science of the singular', CARE Occasional Paper no. 10, University of East Anglia. **11**

Stake, R. E. (1975), *Evaluating the Arts in Education: A Responsive Approach*, Columbus, Ohio, Merrill. **197**

Stake, R. E. (1976), 'Programme evaluation, particularly responsive evaluation', in Dockerell, W. B., Hamilton, D. (eds), *Rethinking Educational Research,* London, Hodder & Stoughton. **69, 134, 164, 197**

Stufflebeam, D. L. (ed.) (1971), *Educational Evaluation and Decision-Making*, Itasca, Peacock. **164**

Tawney, D. (ed.) (1973), *Evaluation in Curriculum Development: Twelve Case Studies,* London, Macmillan. **1**

Taylor, W. (1969), *Society and the Education of Teachers*, London, Faber. **157**

Tyler, R. W. (1971), *Basic Principles of Curriculum and Instruction*, University of Chicago. **165**

Tyler, R., Gagné, R. and Scriven, M. (1967), *Perspectives of Curriculum Evaluation*, AERA Monograph, Chicago, Rand McNally. **164**

Walker, R. (1980), 'The uses of fiction in educational evaluation', *Research into Evaluation*, vol. 2, North West Regional Educational Laboratory, Portland, Oregon. **195**

Walkley, H. (1979), 'Evaluation in the CNAA curriculum process: a case study', *Evaluation Newsletter*, vol. 3, no. 2. **170**

Weber, M. (1964), *The Theory of Social and Economic Organisations*, London, Collier-MacMillan. **152**

Weiner, N. (1968), *The Human Use of Human Beings*, London, Sphere. **173**

Whalley, G. E. (1980), *Teacher Education for Primary School Teachers: Two New Courses and their Evaluation*, University of Leeds School of Education. **95**

Wicksteed, D. (1981), 'Periodic focussing: a model for monitoring courses', *Evaluation Newsletter*, vol. 5, no. 2. **170**

Wilcox, B. and Eustace, P. J. (1981), *Tooling up for Curriculum Review*, Slough, NFER. **10**

Wildavsky, A. (1979), *Speaking Truth to Power: The Art and Craft of Policy Analysis*, Boston, Little, Brown & Co. **180**

Williams, G. (1981), 'Don't overdo the self-recrimination', *Times Higher Education Supplement*, no. 467. **190**

Williams, R. (1976), *Keywords: A Vocabulary of Culture and Society*, Fontana. **151**

Willis, G. (ed.) (1978), *Qualitative Evaluation: Concepts and Cases in Curriculum Criticism*, Berkeley, McCutchan. **101**

Wyatt, J. F. (1977), '"Collegiality" during a period of rapid change in higher education: an examination of a distinctive feature claimed by a group of colleges of education during the 1960s and 1970s'. *Oxford Review of Education*, vol. 3, no. 2. **174**

INDEX

DATE DUE